TOMMY
GEMMELL

TOMMY GEMMELL
Lion Heart

Tommy Gemmell &
Graham McColl

To everyone who helped me throughout my career,
too numerous to mention,
and also to the magical Lisbon Lyons

First published in Great Britain in 2004 by
Virgin Books Ltd
Thames Wharf Studios
Rainville Road
London
W6 9HA

ISBN 1 85227 240 6

Typeset by TW Typesetting, Plymouth, Devon
Printed and bound in Great Britain by
Mackays of Chatham PLC

CONTENTS

FOREWORD by Jimmy Johnstone

Tommy Gemmell was by my side from the very first step that I took in my Celtic career. We met when we both signed for Celtic on the same night and, during the early stages of our careers at the club, Tommy and I and some other young Celtic players from Lanarkshire had a routine, set in stone, of going to a café called Bunty's on Tuesday and Thursday evenings after training, before taking the same bus back to Lanarkshire together. Those were happy times and we all became very friendly whilst we were youngsters.

We progressed to become full-time players at Celtic and, once Tommy had bought his first car, there were no more buses for us. He used to pick me up on the way into training and it was great to drive into Celtic Park in style with Tommy at the wheel. At that time, I was sleeping on a fold-down bed-settee that doubled up as a couch in my parents' front room and, when Tommy arrived outside our home, he would sound the car-horn to let me know he was there and ready to collect me. Sometimes, I would have been lying asleep but, when I heard the horn, I would just pop my head up above the bed-settee as if I had been ready and waiting for him all morning. I would then have to scramble around and get my things together before rushing out to Tommy's car.

Tommy was the original raiding full-back and it was always an exciting sight to see him thundering down the left wing on the overlap. We knew that with him in the side we were always good for a goal. He helped us forwards because, with Tommy in the team, the other side's defence had one more very real danger to worry about. They had to watch him when he got within about 30 yards of goal, and that really stretched defences. There was nobody to match Tommy when we were playing together, although nowadays Roberto Carlos, the Brazilian left-back, is the same type of player, the kind of defender that people will pay to see.

I was one of the first players Tommy recruited when he became manager of Dundee but it was a funny situation. Tommy was there to do a job and make an impression as a young manager but I was playing out my career. It was a difficult time in my life and I have to say that my heart was not in it. I felt bad about the way things eventually turned out. I thought I could get away with doing certain things because Tommy was my friend as well as my manager and I took advantage of that situation. It was not right to do that when Tommy was trying to establish himself in management and I am glad that the situation was resolved quickly. It was my fault things did not work out for me and Tommy at Dens Park. I was pleased to see him go on and do a very good job as manager of Dundee.

Tommy improved tremendously as a player over the years through working hard at his game, but once the hard work in training was over he enjoyed a laugh and a joke. He is just the same nowadays and it is great to see him on each and every occasion when we get together. He is a terrific big guy and, like all the guys I played with, he is always close to my heart.

Jimmy Johnstone
June 2004

PROLOGUE – STRIKING GOLD

I was in the wrong place at the wrong time when I scored the most important goal in my career, for Celtic in the 1967 European Cup final. That was in theory; in reality, I was in exactly the right place at exactly the right time. I had broken one of our manager Jock Stein's golden rules and, although he was probably furious with me at first, he couldn't say much when my gamble paid off and tilted the match in our favour. Big Jock always tried to keep an eye on me because he knew that I was one of the most likely to bend and break his rules, but on this occasion he could not criticise me as my defiance of his orders had brought such spectacular results.

Before my goal, we had been 1–0 down to Internazionale of Milan with more than an hour of the match played and, although we had had 95 per cent of the play, the Italians were holding out in defence, if only just. It was then that I noticed my fellow full-back Jim Craig making a free run with the ball down the right-hand side, so I just set off on a run of my own from our half. Now I should never have done that, because the golden rule was that if Jim Craig was going forward, I was supposed to be keeping the back door shut, along with Billy McNeill and John Clark. But sometimes rules are made to be broken. At that stage of the game Inter were playing with only one man up, Sandro Mazzola, so, with Billy, John and Ronnie Simpson, our goalkeeper, there at the back, there was no point in me hanging back and doing nothing.

I was on the edge of our centre circle and there was nobody in front of me, so I just made a bee-line through Inter's midfield and defence. I ran right through the middle of the park and no Italian player picked me up. It was unbelievable. The guy that was supposed to be on me was Angelo Domenghini but he was a lazy so-and-so. Three times I shouted to Jim Craig to square it, but he held it ... and held it ... and held it. I was beginning to get exasperated with him, because I thought he was never going to cut it back to me and I was getting to the stage where I couldn't go any further. You can only run so far and then you've got to stop. He drew one defender to him, then another, and, when he drew that defender out, he finally decided to cut the ball back to me.

It was only a ten- or twelve-yard pass; that was how close I was to him as he cut it back to me diagonally. I would have been about 25 yards out when I was screaming for it so by the time it got to me I was about 22 or 23 yards out, slightly right of centre, on the arc, the 'D' marking the penalty area. It was a great pass, right along the deck, and the park was like a bowling green, so it was just a matter of timing. I was still making my run and the ball was on the deck when I hit it with my instep, latching on to it cleanly and at full tilt.

An Inter defender, Armando Picchi, had come out to block the ball as I prepared to shoot but about two yards from me he stopped and turned his back. All he had to do was take one more pace and he would have blocked the shot but, as the Italians often do, he came out so far and then turned his back. That gave me a free shot at goal. He may also have blinded his goalkeeper, Giuliano Sarti, slightly when he came out to shut me out, and that would have given Sarti less chance of getting to the ball. Shooting, basically, is all about timing. I just wanted to hit the ball as straight and hard as I could, and when I did I was confident that it was on target. I got right over the top of it and, although it was wide of the 'keeper, I don't think it was above shoulder-height. My momentum took me past Picchi and by that time the ball was in the net.

The first thing I said to myself was, 'That's it. We've got them now.' The Inter players chucked it as soon as I got that goal. You could see their looks of bewilderment. Their hands hit their hips and their heads drooped. As long as we didn't score, they felt they were winning the European Cup but they knew that if we got a goal there would be no way back for them. You could see defeat in their faces.

I had my socks at my ankles because of the heat and there was about half an hour to go. It was roasting. You couldn't get a breath; there wasn't even a breeze. When I went back for the restart and into the left-back position it made me the closest man to the dugout and big Jock Stein said, 'Take it easy, we'll take them in extra time.' I said, 'Fuck that, boss. It's eighty-five degrees out here and the sweat is pouring off us. I'm not playing for another half an hour. We're going to beat them now.'

1. GOOD CLEAN FUN

I spent the best years of my boyhood being tutored in the finest football academy for which a youngster could have wished. It was called Craigneuk, the little Lanarkshire town where I was raised, which is halfway between Motherwell and Wishaw. The environment was perfect for any youngster like me who was enthralled by the game of football. There were dozens of other youngsters willing to play the game from morning to night, seven days a week, without ever tiring of it. You also had to learn to keep your wits about you to survive daily life in Craigneuk, so, all in all, it was a perfect preparation for the rigours and demands of life as a professional footballer.

I was born on 16 October 1943 at my granny's house in Cumbrae Drive in Motherwell, down in the Loaning area behind Motherwell Town Hall. We lived with my granny for five years because my mother and father couldn't get a house of their own. We then moved from my granny's to live with one of my aunties in Airbles Road in Motherwell, just a couple of hundred yards from the football ground – Fir Park. We stayed there for another two years. As usual, in those days, the house had only an outside toilet. Toilet paper was a luxury, so one of my first jobs in life, as a nipper, was to cut up newspapers into suitable sized pieces. There were no lights in the outside toilets and during a Scottish winter they were unbelievably cold. You wouldn't want to go out to them during the night, so when we lived with my auntie we would use a chamber pot. The outside toilet was shared with neighbours and there would be a rota for cleaning it, so the state it was in depended on whom you were sharing it with and their ability as cleaners. It could be horrendous. Still, it never did us any harm.

When I was about seven we got our first house of our own, a prefab in Meadowhead Road, Craigneuk. Our new house had an inside toilet – oh, it was magnificent – but there wasn't a bathroom, so we used a tin bath in front of a coal fire. There was no central heating. Our family then numbered six: I had been my parents' first child but by the time we moved to Craigneuk I had a brother and two sisters; the next oldest is Moira, then David and Anna. We had only two bedrooms, so my brother and I slept in one bed, and my two sisters in another, in one room, while my mother and father slept in the other room. It was pretty cramped but we were at the age when it didn't really matter. Either the guys got up first or the girls did. I suppose it got a wee bit awkward as you got a wee bit older but you were stuck with it. At least it was a lot better than what we had had at my aunt's, where we had all been sharing one room and an alcove.

My father Alfie was a turner at Dalziel steelworks in Motherwell and spent his entire working life there. He was a very quiet man. My mother Margaret was the stronger one, it was she who would chastise us most often, so that we would do the right thing and work at school. If we were needing a clip across the ear, she would be the one to do it. My old man very seldom did that; I can recall him losing his temper only two or three times. But if you saw him getting worked up, you knew to back off. My mother had various jobs: she worked as a petrol pump attendant, did weekly collections for penny policies offered by the Co-op's insurance company and also worked at one of the first garages in Motherwell to have a shop and do-it-yourself pumps. Before we went to school, she looked after us during the daytime; once we were of school age she would work during the day. She would still come in at lunchtime to give us our lunch, which would be something like a piece and jam, because we didn't have money to throw about.

My father was one of a family of thirteen, the last to be born and a twin. I inherited my nose from him, and my features are generally similar to his. My mother was a Stewart and was one of four. If you think back to the 1950s and pictures of film stars with curled, permed hair, that was what my mother looked like. All the women at that time had hot rollers and, when they used them, you could smell the hair burning. I vividly remember my mother and auntie doing each other's hair that way. My mother had a roundish face and wasn't a bad-looking woman. Although she had a fierce temper, she was actually a real softie.

My father was more reserved. He wasn't a socialiser, and he rarely drank. At New Year, we would go to my auntie's after the bells at midnight, and my auntie would pour him a sweet stout at half past midnight; when we left at four in the morning half of it would still be sitting in his glass. The reason was that half of his stomach had been taken away, I think because of stomach ulcers. I can remember my mother taking me into Glasgow Royal Infirmary to see him; that would have been when I was four or five. He hadn't been much of a drinker before but after that he just made up his mind to moderate his consumption of alcohol.

My parents taught us discipline. If you are taught discipline when you are a youngster it stays with you right through your life. I have always respected the law and have never become involved in any criminal activity. It was a good grounding we were given by our parents: we were taught respect for other people and their property. There's no such a thing as a bad kid: there are only bad parents.

We had only the basics in terms of furniture: a table and chairs, beds. We had one set of clothes each, more or less – maybe a spare pair of trousers and a spare shirt and sweater – one pair of shoes, and a pair of sandshoes, or gutties as we called them, in which we could run about. I can remember going to school with holes in the soles of my shoes and two pieces of cardboard inside to protect my feet from the damp, nothing else, until my father could get hold of the leather to repair the shoes. It was a fairly ordinary, basic type of life and upbringing, nothing fancy, just the same as everybody around us. We were lucky that my old man never missed a day's work in his life, and my mother always had a job, either full-time or part-time, because she and my father needed all the money they could get to pay the rent and bring up four kids.

I used to have to go to the butcher's on a Saturday morning. There would be a queue 50 or 60 yards long outside, so I had to wait in the queue, pay the tick from the previous week, as noted in the butcher's book, and get whatever my mother wanted that day. Then, each day during the week, one of the family would go to the butcher's for that day's meat and get it put in the book again. Every trader had a tick book, and if you didn't pay them on a Saturday morning that was that: you didn't get anything else from them. Our normal breakfast would maybe be a boiled egg and toast or a piece and strawberry jam; we could not afford bacon and eggs or anything like that. For lunch it would be the same again and for dinner, mince and tatties or bangers and mash – stuff like that. It was very basic but you never starved. There was always plenty of bread and tatties but you didn't get anything exotic. At least, not often. I can distinctly remember my mother coming in one day with a melon. We had never seen one before. I said, 'What's that?' She said, 'It's a wee treat.' So she cut it up. It was rare to see fruit such as that but I didn't like it. She said, 'Eat it. You're not getting anything else.'

My father got a fortnight's holiday in the summer; that was his only break from work other than Christmas Day, Boxing Day and two days at New Year. We went six years in succession to Girvan for our summer holidays, and six years on the trot my old man took me to the pictures, and six years on the trot it was the same movie: *The Jolson Story*, starring Al Jolson. I'd say, 'Dad, we're not going to see that again. We saw that last year.' There would be no stopping him, though. 'It's a great film,' he'd say and off we'd go. There must have been a lot of people of the same mind for the picture house to have put it on every summer. We then went six years in succession to Aberdeen. We always stayed in digs; never in bed-and-breakfast accommodation or hotels. So you had one or two rooms of the landlady's house to yourself. When we went to Aberdeen, the football season had started and we would usually see a couple of Aberdeen matches while we were up there. Otherwise, it would be the usual holiday stuff: playing on the beach, sandcastles, seagulls shitting on your head.

At Christmas, you would be doing well to get a present of any description. If you were lucky, you'd get the *Oor Wullie* or *The Broons* annual and your stocking filled with sweeties and maybe a toy of some sort. As I got older, my mother would give my brothers and sisters hand-me-downs; my brother would maybe get a toy train that I had had previously. There would be no turkey and trimmings for us at Christmas: it would be plain, normal, basic grub, nothing special – soup, steak pie and tatties. If we were lucky we might get chicken. Birthdays would be nothing special either. You would get a card from your mother and father: end of story.

My most vivid early memories are of school buses and school dinners. You were picked up every day by a free bus and got free school meals, which I loved. I went to Craigneuk Primary School and had my first game for the school's football team when I was about eight years old. I played wearing a pair of Wellington boots because we couldn't afford football boots and wellies were about the nearest thing I had. You can imagine the big red rims round my legs after playing a match in Wellington boots. Eventually, my father got me a pair of football boots. He had a cobbler's last in the house and soled and heeled all the family's shoes because we couldn't afford to go to the cobbler's or to buy new shoes. He became very skilful; he had a hasp and mended heels and soles unbelievably well. So, given how tight finances were at home, I considered myself lucky when I was given a second-hand pair of football boots, even though they were two sizes too big for me.

At that time boots had individual leather studs, each with three nails in it, each nail about three quarters of an inch long. They were broad at the bottom and tapered to about a quarter of an inch at the top. My old man used to hammer all these studs into my football boots and use his cobbler's last to flatten the nails into the sole of the boot as they came through. Once you started wearing the boots, though, the nails loosened and you would end up getting cut feet because of the nails piercing the sole. Each time, my father would get the boots back on to the last to flatten the studs, but they would always come loose again and you would always end a match with cut feet. I shudder to think about the number of cuts you got in your legs when you played in schools football at that time, because when the leather wore down in the stud itself the nails would start to protrude, so that when you went into tackles, the nails in other players' studs would lacerate your legs. It was good for toughening us up, though.

We didn't have much else to do in Craigneuk other than play football. At home we had an old, old radio, or wireless, as it was called at that time, and I remember listening to the Top 20 on Radio Luxembourg early on a Sunday evening. That was the only time I really listened to it, but my mother would listen a lot. She was in her early twenties when I was born, so she was still young when I was growing up, and she listened to all the hit records of the day: Bill Haley and the Comets, Frank Sinatra, Dean Martin, Nat King Cole and Cliff Richard, who was breaking through at that time – mainly melodies but with a wee bit of rock 'n' roll in there as well. We couldn't afford a record player so she relied on the radio, and terrible squeaks and screeching used to come out of it sometimes, maybe halfway through a record, because it had old-fashioned valves and was on its last legs. We didn't have a television when I was a young boy but I can remember going to a neighbour's house to see what I believe was the first floodlit match played in Scotland: Clyde playing Wolverhampton Wanderers. At that time Wolves had a great side with Billy Wright, Ron Flowers and Bert Williams, the goalkeeper. That neighbour was the only one in our wee cul-de-sac of six detached prefabs who had a television. When anything like that was on, everybody went into their house. Eventually, we got a telly, a second-hand job. That would have been in the late '50s, when I was around thirteen, and we thought we were the bee's knees. We never had a telephone all the time we lived in that prefab.

For games, other than football, we would do things like make our own bows and arrows by cutting branches off trees and using a knife to sharpen the arrows. It was a happy childhood. Everybody did the same things: hide and seek, all that sort of stuff. Then, when we got a bit older, we used to go down to an orchard and steal apples and pears, or steal turnips and tatties out of folk's gardens and then build a wee fire on waste ground and throw the tatties and turnips on to it. They would come out all black and when you ate them you ended up looking like Al Jolson. We would often be caught and get a boot on the arse from the farmer or the person whose garden we had raided.

I also got caught a few times playing football in the street. It's funny: nowadays people say that one of the reasons we no longer have such great players in Scotland is that boys no longer play football in the street. The thing is, when I was a boy, you were never actually *meant* to play football in the street – for your own safety, in case you got hit by a vehicle. Anyway, we played in the street all the time. Sometimes we didn't have a ball so we just played with a tin can. You would go to play football in the street and before you knew it, the cops would nip round the corner and grab you. You froze as soon as they said, 'Don't move!' Everybody was terrified of the cops because it was driven into you not to get into any bother with the police, so you had a natural fear of authority. You were told that you could get locked up in the bad boys' school and we knew boys to whom that did happen. That would be for serious stuff like thieving, though, and we never did any serious thieving or kicking in windows or doors or anything like that.

We also used to play cards – maybe pontoon but for no money – in derelict buildings and the cops would come up with their batons drawn and give you a boot on the arse. It was actually for your own good because those buildings could have collapsed at any time. That was when I was about eight or nine years old. The cops would take your address and go to your house and tell your parents where they had found you. Then, the next time you went in, you would get a boot on the arse from your old man or a skelp across the jaw from your mother. Like most working-class people, they saw it as a stigma to have the police at the door of the family home.

One day whilst playing football in the street I was hit by a van. It caught me a glancing blow on my backside. You were supposed to stop and let a van past but I didn't see it because we were busy playing. I had to limp along to the house, which was about 100 yards away. My old man said, 'What happened to you?' I said, 'I was playing football in the street and got hit on my backside by a van.' He wasn't exactly sympathetic: he gave me a boot on the arse, on the other side from where I had been struck by the van. 'That's evened it up,' he said. 'You've got a proper sore arse now.'

Craigneuk was a hard, hard place in which to be raised. There were rival teenage gangs only three or four streets away from where we lived. I kept out of their road and never got involved but I saw them going about with cleavers, sickles and all sorts of other weapons. There was a hard core that made sure there were always gang-fights in Craigneuk. You had to keep your nose clean: if you joined a gang, you could be sure that the other two or three gangs were looking for you, so I had nothing to do with any of them; as soon as I saw them I would disappear. There was quite a lot of violence; I saw two or three gang-fights in the street, maybe a couple of hundred yards away from me. In the papers next day there would be stories about people having had their ears cut off in these fierce battles. Thankfully, they kept it to their own part of town, the top end, the Wishaw side, and I lived on the Motherwell side.

The main street in Craigneuk would probably be about a mile long and the town was about half a mile wide. The streets backed on to the Ravenscraig steelworks and were lined with old tenements with outside toilets and communal outdoor wash-houses with great big tubs, around two feet square, for people to do their washing in, using the old washboards. You had to watch your washing because if somebody saw your shirt out on the line they would nick it if they got a chance. There was still a good community spirit in Craigneuk; the hooligans kept to their own type and the decent folk kept to theirs. I can't remember us ever falling out with neighbours. Nowadays you've got folk in detached houses and they won't talk to their neighbours across the garden wall but we got to know them all. Most people lived in tenements so they knew each other from sharing outside toilets and tubs at the steamie.

Then there would be the bookie's runner on the street corner, because bookies were illegal at that time. The bookie's runner would take your bets and money and then take them down to the bookie and put them on. My old man got nabbed a couple of times for dealing with a bookie's runner. The bookie's house was used as a betting shop; the cops knew what was going on and would raid it now and again, just to keep up appearances, and everyone who was caught inside would be fined £1. My old man liked a wee punt and was caught in there a couple of times but the bookie always paid his customers' fines and the whole thing would start all over again.

Although football took up much of my time, I still won the Dux medal at Craigneuk Primary School. Equally importantly, as it seemed to me, we won the Motherwell and Wishaw Primary School League trophy. Before you left primary school, you had to sit the eleven-plus examination, the result of which would determine which secondary school you attended. The eleven-plus was feared because at that early stage in your life it could do an enormous amount to determine what would happen to you later. If you failed, you went to a school which concentrated on technical subjects and you were almost certainly destined to become a manual worker; if you passed, you would go to a school where they focused on academic subjects and you had a strong chance of becoming a white-collar worker. I was quite happy in the run-up to it because we had had monthly exams in writing, spelling and arithmetic and I always passed them without any problems. As I had won the Dux medal out of the 40 pupils in our year, and all of us were crammed into the same classroom, I knew whom I was competing with and I was quite confident of success in the eleven-plus. I passed it with flying colours and went to Wishaw High School, a senior secondary; those with a lower mark in the eleven-plus went to Wishaw Central School, a junior secondary.

At Wishaw High School I got even more involved in playing football, and academic subjects began to take a back seat. I also had a paper run in the morning, for which I would rise at six o'clock, and a Lipton's grocery run after school, for which I had one of the shop's bikes with a basket on the front. So with the football and my two part-time jobs, I had little time for homework. I would try to get my homework done after my paper round and before I cycled to school, which was about three miles away, or scramble to do it in the classroom before the teacher entered to begin that day's lesson. At primary school, I had studied. That was how I had won the Dux medal; my mother would tell me I wasn't going down the park to play football until I had done my homework. At night, in those early school years, I would do my homework, have a quick bite to eat and then go down the park to play football until it was dark.

Having so few luxuries and distractions at home, we got most of our enjoyment from playing football. Once we had graduated to having a proper laced-up football to play with, we had started going down to the public park and there was no more football in the street. On evenings after school about twenty of us would put our jackets down and play football until it was dark. During summer nights we would go to the park at five o'clock and still be playing football at half past ten, by which time the scoreline would be 44–all or something like that. That was probably the best background you could have if you wanted to be a footballer. We would not worry about our homework – *that* was our homework. Nowadays, if you pass a public park in Scotland, you will very rarely see youngsters playing football, and maybe that's why the Scottish national side is in the mess it's in at the moment.

In another football-based game that we used to play, four or five of us hit a ball against a tenement's gable end and each guy was given the name of a team. As soon as you hit the ball against the gable end, you shouted out the name of a team and the player who had been given that team name was supposed to take just one touch to hit the ball off the wall; he wasn't allowed to control it. He would then shout out the name of another team and another player would have to go for the ball, using his left or right foot, whichever was best for hitting the ball back off the wall. Now that sharpened up your reactions and control. It was a good grounding – nobody gave us any coaching in how to pass or control a ball or how to shoot or head or anything. You just had to teach yourself and the more you did it the easier it became.

As a schoolboy footballer for Wishaw High, I played outside-right for the junior and intermediate teams. I never got a chance to get in a lot of shots at goal in those days as all I was doing was sticking in crosses. So I had no idea then that I had the potential to be a goal scorer. I was also playing against guys who eventually signed for Celtic. One was Bobby Murdoch, who was playing for Our Lady's High School in Motherwell. They also had John Cushley, Tom Duddy and Jim Conway, the centre-forward, all of whom also signed for Celtic. They were the best team by far in schools football in the Lanarkshire area at that time but we always seemed to beat them. Bobby played against me in the junior side and then their intermediate side. I also remember that when I was playing for Wishaw High's intermediate team, Billy McNeill was playing for Our Lady's senior team and someone told me he was signing for Celtic. You could see why: in the air, he was absolutely fantastic. The Celtic scout for Lanarkshire at that time was Eddie McArdle, who later became Lord Provost of Motherwell and Wishaw, and the number of players he took from Our Lady's High School to Celtic was nobody's business.

When I got to fourteen, I was playing not only for the school but also for an amateur side called Meadow Thistle, so named because the guys who formed the committee all lived on Meadowhead Road, as I did; I was one of the founder members of the club, which played in the Lanarkshire Under-18 Amateur League. I was usually too young to get a game but when they were short of players they stuck me in and I played on the right wing. One day, when I was fifteen, they were short of a full-back and stuck me in at left-back. I was quite comfortable hitting the ball with my left or my right peg because of all the time I had spent hitting that ball against that gable end in my earlier years, and I quickly became a regular in the side. As a boy, I wasn't very well-built; in fact, I was quite slight. At fifteen, I was about five feet four inches tall but by the time I was eighteen I was six feet one. During my early amateur days I was constantly being brushed aside, so I wasn't a lot of good to the team. I was just another body. Then I started sprouting and getting a bit broader and stronger.

I did like some subjects at secondary school, such as arithmetic, geometry, geography and history, and I was fine with physical education but I hated other subjects like algebra and logarithms and just switched off in those classes, so I wasn't getting very good marks but I was scraping through. I hated my algebra teacher. He had one of those dusters with a wooden base that they used to wipe clean the blackboard, and, if you were looking down at your desk and not paying attention, he would launch it at you across the classroom. He had perfect aim and, if the wooden bit struck you on the head, it was too bad. There was also a woodwork teacher who, if you made a mess of something, would make you lean over the desk, take a plank of wood and batter you across the backside with it three or four times. The pain was unbelievable. Apart from those two maniacs, the teachers were all right.

If I had been rubbish at football, I would probably have stuck in at school a bit more. Even so, at the age of sixteen, I could have stayed on at school if I had wanted to, because I had obtained the appropriate grades, but my old man said they were looking for apprentices at the Ravenscraig steelworks, which had recently opened and which belonged to David Colville & Sons, who also owned the steelworks at which my father was employed. The personnel people at his work had put up notices saying that apprenticeships were available at Ravenscraig and anyone who had a son who might be suitable should have him apply. Employers of Colville & Sons – so long as they were highly rated as workers – would get the first chance of putting their sons' names down.

So I went down to Dalziel steelworks for an interview. My father told me that I should take the chance of an apprenticeship because he and my mother knew I was struggling at school, since I was playing more football than I had ever played in my life. After a second interview, I was offered an apprenticeship. I could have taken my pick and trained as an engineer, an electrician or an instrument mechanic; a whole gamut of trades was available. I decided to become a sparky, an electrician, and the tools and facilities were brand-new and bang up-to-date. It was quite a prize for a lad like me from a working-class background. So far as the company was concerned, they believed they were getting a good worker because, they thought, if the father was conscientious, the son would be as well.

We started at seven o'clock and finished at half past four. I had been given a bike by my parents for winning the Dux medal and, when I was sixteen and starting to serve my apprenticeship at Ravenscraig, the company sent me to Mossend steelworks, the training school, for six months. I was using this school bike, that I had been given when I was twelve, to cycle four miles or so up and down hills to Mossend and my knees were hitting the handlebars. As with so many youngsters in the late 50s and early 60s, that time of full employment, my life looked as though it was already mapped out for me, even though I was still only in my mid-teens. But then, just as everything looked set to take an utterly predictable shape, my life began to develop in a manner I had never dreamed possible.

2. FOLLOWING MY FEET

Throughout my boyhood years there had been only one team I had wanted to play for: Motherwell. I had been one of the thousands who had lined the streets to acclaim the Motherwell team that had won the Scottish Cup by beating Dundee 4–0 in the 1952 final, and Motherwell was the only senior team for whom I wanted to sign. I couldn't see past them. They were my home-town club and my old man used to take me to all their games, in the days when you could lift kids over the turnstiles. So I was a Motherwell fanatic. At that time, Motherwell were regularly getting home attendances of anything from 20,000 to 30,000 and I was dying to play for them, so when, in the spring of 1961, I was named in a Lanarkshire Amateur side to play a Glasgow Amateur side at Fir Park, Motherwell's home ground, I saw it as my big opportunity to impress the people at Motherwell Football Club. This was my chance to step into the limelight.

As I had left school at sixteen, I had never reached the senior side at Wishaw High, but I was still playing for a good Meadow Thistle team and that had attracted the attention of the Lanarkshire selectors. So here was I at seventeen, playing at Fir Park in this representative game, and I was up against a guy called John McGuire who had already signed provisional forms for Celtic; if you signed provisionally and you didn't make it, you could always go back to amateur football. On the day, I didn't let John McGuire get a look at the ball and about an hour after I got home from the game, wee Eddie McArdle chapped the door and asked if I would like to go to Celtic Park and do some training two nights a week along with the club's part-time players. He said they would pay my travelling expenses, around 30 bob (£1.50) a week, to travel on buses back and forward from Craigneuk to Celtic Park. I was quite happy with that because, even though I was mad keen to sign for Motherwell, this was a toe in the door to professional football. The sentimental pull of the home-town club was strong but if a club like Celtic gives you an offer to train with them, you don't knock it back. There were loads of guys who never got that opportunity yet were much better players than me. Many of them never got picked up at all, and those who did went to what you might call lesser sides. I asked my father what he thought about Celtic's offer. 'Well,' he said, 'it's an opportunity. It's a chance.'

An English club, Brentford, also wanted me to sign for them at that time. They actually wanted me to sign as a full-time footballer, not to train part-time as Celtic had offered. The offer from Brentford had also stemmed from that match at Fir Park; the day after Eddie McArdle came to our doorstep, Brentford's West of Scotland-based scout did the same. Now I didn't know where Brentford was until somebody told me it was in London. So when they said they would like me to come down for a week to have a wee look about I said to myself, 'London . . . for a week . . . that'll do me. That'll be a nice wee trip to see the bright lights.' I had never been out of Scotland. My old man said to me, 'Have you any intention of signing for them?' I said, 'No.' 'Well,' he said, 'if you have no intention of signing for them, you're not going.' He didn't want me to go down on a freebie just to see London and muck people around. So that was the end of that. I had no intention of signing for Brentford because I had never heard of them and I was still keeping my fingers crossed that Motherwell would sign me.

It was Celtic, though, who had been the Scottish club to come in for me, and, after a few training sessions with the club, an agreement was reached whereby I would train with them on Tuesday and Thursday nights and play on Saturdays for Coltness United, a junior club from the town of Newmains, who played in the Lanarkshire junior League. I signed for Coltness United, on an amateur form, one night and, on the following night, I signed a provisional form for Celtic. Coltness had to sign and register me first, and then Celtic on the following day. If I had not followed that procedure, I would not have been able to go back to Junior or amateur football if I had failed to make it at Celtic. That was in October 1961 and another youngster signed his provisional forms on the same Thursday night as me; his name was Jimmy Johnstone. We were signed by Jimmy McGrory, the manager, and Sean Fallon, assistant to the manager. They told us that all we had at that point was potential, but that if we stuck in at the game and kept improving we could go places.

Wee Jimmy and I had actually met previously – we had both been at Burnbank Technical College in Lanarkshire on day release from our apprenticeships. Wee Jimmy was training to be a welder and I was serving my apprenticeship to become a sparky. We would have a kickaround in the grounds of the college at break-time, playing with a tennis ball. Jimmy, even at sixteen, was unbelievable. It was impossible to get that tennis ball away from him. I said to myself when I first saw him in those kickarounds, 'Who is this?' Wee Jinky could already do everything he would do when he was 21 or 22 and a fully fledged member of the first team. He told me he had been into Celtic Park, talking to them and doing a bit of training, just as I had. On the night we both signed provisionally, he and I and our fathers took the same bus back to Lanarkshire. Jimmy got off at Viewpark and we went back to Craigneuk.

I was still serving my apprenticeship at Ravenscraig as a sparky, starting at seven o'clock in the morning, and on Tuesdays and Thursdays at half past four I'd go straight from Ravenscraig on to the bus for Parkhead Cross and seven times out of ten I would fall asleep and wake up at Glasgow Cross with no money to get the tramcar back to Celtic Park – so I would have to run the distance. I didn't find the schedule too demanding; I was young and getting stronger by the day, had a lot of enthusiasm and knew I was being given an opportunity to do something with my life. At that time there would be about 20 unsigned guys like myself there for training twice a week, with a dozen who had been signed as part-timers. Billy McNeill was one of those signed part-timers – he worked with an insurance broker and trained with us on Tuesday and Thursday nights. He was so outstanding that he had become established in Celtic's first team a couple of years earlier, despite being a part-time footballer.

Coltness United had been sniffing around Meadow Thistle for a while before I signed for them. Playing for them on Saturdays was handy because they were only four miles up the road from Craigneuk. It was quite funny: even though I had signed an amateur form for Coltness, they gave me an envelope every match day with a ten-bob (50p) note inside it. It was funnier still that, whilst I was getting ten bob a week, the semi-professionals at Coltness were getting seven bob and a tanner (37p). Coltness had also told me when they had been trying to sign me that I would get half of any money that they might get from Celtic for compensation. So, when I signed provisionally for Celtic, Coltness got £70 from them as a sweetener, to soften the blow in case Coltness might lose me after just one season. Immediately Coltness came up with the £35 that was my share. There had also been a signing-on fee from Celtic of £20. So I had received £20 from Celtic and £35 from Coltness United and I was earning ten bob a week from Coltness, £2 a week from Celtic for travelling expenses and my wages from Ravenscraig, which were £4 17 shillings and a tanner; just short of a fiver. So I had £55 in the bank and was getting more than seven pounds a week, at a time when you could go out with ten or fifteen bob in your pocket and it would last you a week. Already, in a small way, I was enjoying a taste of the delights of playing football professionally.

At two or three Coltness games I spied Sean Fallon on the terracing. He was checking on my progress and on that of another Coltness player whom Celtic had as a provisional signing, a guy called Bobby Jeffrey. We had a good side at Coltness and reached the quarter-finals of the Scottish Junior Cup before Rob Roy knocked us out: they beat us 1–0 at their home ground in Kirkintilloch and went on to win the Cup that year. I played just one season with Coltness – 1961–62 – because Celtic decided I should become what you might describe as a full-time part-timer: a part-time player but with no commitments to any other club.

I quickly became a regular with Celtic's third team, which was run by John Higgins. Celtic played their third-team matches at Barrowfield, on a red-ash pitch, and we trained on that as well. On numerous occasions I and other players would go into the dressing room with friction burns from this red ash. I can remember Bob Rooney, the trainer, scrubbing my thighs with a nailbrush until they were bleeding, to get all the grit out of them. He would then dab the wound with powder, and the next thing that would happen would be that you had a great big scab. They didn't have the antiseptic fluids that we have nowadays; they just used a nailbrush.

Becoming a regular in Celtic's third team was another significant step towards full-time professional football: Celtic had put me on a three-year contract, which meant I was no longer a provisional signing but a full signing, albeit as a part-time player. The wages were £7 a week but if I played in the first team I would get £18 a week – good money, but still a bit less than the established first-team players, who at that time were getting £30 a week. The bonus was restricted to £3 for a win and 30 bob for a draw, the maximum allowed by the SFA (Scottish Football Association). That was at the beginning of the 1962–63 season, by which time my wages at Ravenscraig had increased to £6 per week. So I was feeling flush.

I had played only seven or eight games in the third team when I started getting a semi-regular game in the reserve team. That was still in my first full season at the club, 1962–63, and my progress continued quite smoothly after I became a regular for the reserves. Soon I was ready for my first-team debut, even though I was still a part-time player, training on Tuesdays and Thursdays.

My debut for Celtic's first team was at Pittodrie Stadium, Aberdeen, on 5 January 1963, just over a year after I had joined the club. Substitutions were still not allowed in the Scottish game at that time so there was no prospect of easing young players into the first team via the substitutes' bench. My opportunity knocked when Jim Kennedy, the first-choice left-back, and Willie O'Neill, the second-choice man for that position, were both injured. So my name was listed on the noticeboard in the dressing room as a member of the party that was to travel to Aberdeen for the match at Pittodrie. As I was still part-time, it was only when I went into training on the Thursday evening that I saw my name up on the noticeboard as part of the pool of players that was to go north on the Friday to stay in the Bay Hotel in Stonehaven prior to the match. That was enough of a big deal for me but on the Friday evening I got a phone call at eight o'clock at night. The guy on the other end informed me that he was from the *Aberdeen Evening Express*, said he had heard that I was playing in the Celtic first team on the following day and wondered whether he could get a wee story and a picture for the paper. So I said I would need to speak to the manager, Mr McGrory. As always, he was puffing away on his pipe, looking as content as your grandfather on Christmas Day. He said, 'That's all right, son, no problem.' So half an hour later I was standing outside the hotel awaiting this guy from the *Aberdeen Evening Express*, and you can imagine what that was like on a freezing cold early January evening in the North-East. Half an hour later I was still standing there waiting for this guy when Paddy Crerand came out and said, 'Get yourself in here. Have you not even realised we've been carrying out a spoof on you?' I had been standing there, cold but excited, dreaming of the spotlight, and visualising my picture and story in the paper.

I played right-back that day at Pittodrie and we beat Aberdeen 5–1. Three weeks later I played again for the first team in a midweek Scottish Cup tie against Falkirk at Brockville and the ground was as hard as a table. I went down on my knee and nicked my cartilage and the knee just swelled up like a balloon. So that was me out of business for about three weeks and by that time Jim Kennedy had returned to the team at left-back so I had to suffer in silence. I played only one more first-team game during the 1962–63 season, but in the following season – 1963–64 – I was to become more or less a regular.

Bob Kelly, the chairman, picked the team at that time and I was fortunate in that he seemed to like me. Jimmy McGrory had been manager for close to twenty years but by 1963 he had little influence in the running of the club. Sean Fallon, who had become assistant to the manager by the time I made my debut, was Bob Kelly's right-hand man. Celtic had a board meeting at Celtic Park every Thursday night and Jimmy McGrory submitted a team. If Bob Kelly agreed with it, that was the team. If he didn't agree with it, didn't like one or two of the players that Jimmy McGrory had selected, he would change it and put in the players that he wanted. Everyone knew that Jimmy McGrory was merely a figurehead, Bob Kelly was pulling the strings and that Sean

Fallon was ensuring that Kelly's orders were carried out. Bob Kelly loved Celtic and because he never had a family, Celtic was his family. He and Desmond White owned most of the shares in the club and everything that Bob Kelly did, whether right or wrong, he did for the right reasons and for what he thought would benefit Celtic. He made a lot of bad decisions but he also made a lot of good ones, such as bringing in the youngsters in the early 60s and phasing out the guys who were getting a wee bit past it and had done their bit.

Celtic has never been a Catholic club and never in my life have I thought of it as such. It was founded, back in 1888, by people who were of an Irish Catholic background, and the club has had a lot of tremendous Catholic players, but they have also had a lot of tremendous Protestant players, and players of other religions, stretching back across the decades. If you look at Celtic, if only in the years immediately before I joined the club in the early 60s, they had Bobby Evans, Bertie Peacock and Jock Stein as captains and they were all Protestants. These were footballers first and foremost. They didn't go to Celtic to go to chapel; they joined Celtic to play football.

Bob Kelly was a very devout Catholic but he was no bigot. If there was any swearing on the team bus he would have a word in the ear of Sean Fallon, and Sean would say, 'Right, guys, watch the language.' Bob Kelly went to Mass every morning and I have nothing against that but he signed a lot of Protestants in his time at Celtic and I never at any time heard a Celtic director say anything against another religion.

Things were sometimes less proper among certain members of the playing staff. Right at the start of my time at Celtic, there weren't many Protestants on the club's books. Ian Young joined at the same time as me and early in the 1963–64 season we formed a full-back partnership in the first team, with Ian on the right-hand side and me on the left. Ian had replaced Dunky MacKay and I had replaced Jim Kennedy and some of the more experienced players resented us, two Proddies, coming in and taking over from Dunky and Jim, who were big, big favourites in the dressing room. Jim Kennedy, if he was selected for the team, would be pushed forward to allow me to remain at full-back and at other times he would be left out of the starting eleven entirely. In effect, I had taken over from him. At that time Ian and I were the only Proddies in the first team and, if either of us had had a bad game, certain other players might say, 'What do you expect of an Orange bastard?' They would say it directly to you; they were not joking or having a lark. Sometimes, in matches, when things were not working for you, you would hear similar comments from other players in the teams. I don't know why they called me an Orange bastard because I've never been in an Orange Lodge in my life.

I just wanted to go out there and play. I would say, whenever someone started to abuse me verbally, 'I just want a chance to establish myself. Everybody's entitled to a bad game now and then, aren't they?' What else could I say? I don't know why but obviously some players are more bigoted than others and they were the ones who would make comments. A handful of players at the club could be described as real bigots; they would have liked to see a Celtic side that was always 100 per cent Catholic. The rest of the guys were all right; there were no problems whatsoever. Guys like Billy McNeill and Stevie Chalmers were never bigoted. The bigoted guys had been at the club for a while but why they thought the way they did, I don't know, because Celtic had received great service from the likes of Jock Stein, Bertie Peacock and Bobby Evans, who had probably been coming to the end of their time at Celtic when these guys had first joined the club.

During my first full season I wasn't playing brilliantly but I was doing a steady job and I needed encouragement more than criticism. To his credit, Bob Kelly was always keen to stress my merits as a player. As I got more experience, then, like any young player in that situation, I became a better player and a more valuable member of the side. I think that once the other, more senior, players saw that I was doing a wee turn for the team then everything became hunky-dory, but there had been some resentment of me when I was first becoming established.

Celtic don't ever have to lose the Irish connection because you cannot change history; there is no reason why anyone should try to disguise the history of the club and pretend it wasn't founded by a Marist brother. The club was built to raise money for the poor in the East End of Glasgow, and Celtic still do charity work for causes throughout the world, so they have never lost that connection. The club has always made donations to a variety of different charities, not just Catholic ones. In the early '60s, for example, shortly ofter I had joined the club, Celtic once played Real Madrid in a friendly at Celtic Park and got a full house – their biggest midweek attendance up until that time: 76,000. The proceeds went to a Jewish charity.

In my early days at Celtic as a part-timer, our training on Tuesday and Thursday nights consisted of simply going round and round the track. We would see very little of the ball. This would be our training session: one easy lap; one fast lap; two fast laps; ten 220-yard runs; ten 100-yarders; ten 50-yarders; ten 20-yarders. Then, if it was a light spring or summer's night we might be given a wee kick of the ball after we had done all of our track work, a wee seven-a-side game, behind the goals at Celtic Park; at that time, there were short, semi-oval expanses of grass behind both goals. On a winter's night, though there would be just one floodlight on at the ground and we would be told to get straight into the bath after our running sessions. So during the winter we never saw a ball.

My own game was still developing. On reaching sixteen, I had realised that I had the ability to shoot at goal with power and accuracy from distance. It is all about timing; it's just like swinging a golf club or a tennis racket. Look at David Beckham; there is not a pick on him and he is scoring from dead-ball situations with ease so it has nothing to do with having a powerful physique. There were guys at Celtic like big John Cushley, Billy McNeill's understudy, who was as strong as an ox but couldn't burst a paper bag with a shot. His timing when striking a dead ball was shocking but he was a big, steady centre-half.

Uninterrupted upward progress was all I knew at this time. During the second season of my initial three-year contract, 1963–64, I played no fewer than 49 games in the first team; Stevie Chalmers was the only Celtic player to make more first-team appearances. So I was getting £18 a week plus the £3 win bonus, which came our way regularly enough, plus my weekly wage from Ravenscraig, all of which meant I was nearly as well-off as the full-time first-team players.

It is incredible to think that I was playing in front of thousands of people for Celtic in that 1963–64 season, both at home and abroad, a season in which we reached the latter stages of European competition, and was still clocking on every morning for a full daily shift at Ravenscraig. If I was required for midweek matches I just had to beg time off work: if we had an evening match, for example, or a match abroad, I would get days off work in lieu of holidays. The people running Ravenscraig were very good to me, I must admit. The boss of the electrical department, Tam Somerville, was a red-hot football supporter, a Hamilton Accies man, if I remember correctly. He was a smashing guy and knew I had signed provisionally for Celtic so he was very accommodating about allowing me time off work. He also asked me to play unauthorised football for the Ravenscraig electrical department and, after he'd been so good to me, I couldn't very well say no, even though it was strictly against SFA rules for a registered professional to do such a thing. We won the Colville Group trophy and a photograph of our winning team appeared in the works magazine. I was terrified in case somebody at the SFA spied it because they could have suspended or fined me, or both, and at Celtic you didn't get any money when you were suspended. Fortunately, nothing happened and Tam Somerville was delighted by our victory.

At the time I joined Celtic, the club was going through a hard time because Rangers were winning everything. Celtic was rebuilding and a lot of young players were being signed, which opened up opportunities for players such as myself. Bobby Murdoch and Bobby Lennox had signed just before me and Jim Craig around the same time. Jimmy Johnstone, of course, was the standout. He was incredible. Nobody could get the ball off him and yet, for some reason, in his early years at Celtic he wasn't a regular. They played him and then left him out time and again. Maybe that was because he was a more modern type of player than the traditional winger. At that time, wingers were supposed to go down the line and cross the ball for the big centre-forward to nod it into the net, and every team played with two wingers and a big centre-forward. When wee Jinky started playing, though, he was taking on full-backs and pulling out central defenders and cutting it back for someone to knock it into the net; very seldom would he cross the ball from the goal-line.

Jimmy McGrory, the manager, had been the greatest goal scorer in Celtic's history during his playing career but despite what he had done for the club, both as a player and as a manager, he was a very humble, mild-mannered man. He was an office-bound manager. He was there, hovering around inside Celtic Park, on training nights and on match days but you very seldom saw him involved in training. Alec Boden was the trainer for the part-timers, John Higgins looked after the third team and Sean Fallon, Bob Rooney and Neilly Mochan would do the training for the reserves and the first team. Jimmy McGrory would chat to the boys, puff on his pipe, pat you on the back and say, 'You're doing well, son.' He stayed in the background even when you were a full-time player. He would be in the dressing room before the game but there would be little discussion of tactics. Our instructions would be very simple. We had to make sure it was a case of safety first at the back: if the play was on the right-hand side I had to be tucked round the back of defence as a safety valve and it was the same for the guy on the other side. That was the extent of the tactics for the defenders.

If you were a full-back, your job was to get the ball from back to front; you were expected to punt the ball the length of the park in the direction of the winger. If you could mark your opponent, get the ball off of him and hump it 60 or 70 yards from the back to the front, you were termed a good player. You were doing your job. If the wingers were going down the touchline like billyo and firing balls across, they were doing their jobs. If the big centre-forward was up there to head them in, he was doing his job. Midfield players were expected to do little more than tackle in the middle of the park and fire the ball to the front players. Dunky MacKay, a first-teamer with whom I played on a few occasions, was a full-back in advance of his time. He was knocking the ball to the likes of Paddy Crerand in midfield, getting it back and then knocking it to an inside-forward, as they were called in those days, and getting it back, but they didn't like that at Celtic Park. If you wanted to play in the first team, you had to conform to their basic ideas about football. Dunky was a footballing full-back, so he was left out of the team because he was playing too much football.

I was happy because I was playing in the first team but I wasn't happy with their style of play: my instinct was to go forward because in my school and amateur days I had played as a winger. So I was playing against my instincts. I wasn't happy humping the ball forward 70 yards because 70-yard passes were almost always won by opposition defenders. If the other team were humping 60- or 70-yard passes into our defence, Billy McNeill just used to knock them out with ease; nobody could beat him in the air. If a 70-yard ball was played up the wing then I, or Ian Young on the right side, would just knock it away. So you said to yourself, 'Why do we play like that?' At that time, we were taught nothing about teamwork: no one tried to knit us together as a team. Instead, if they thought you were a good enough individual player you would be thrust into the team and left to sink or swim. It was perhaps no surprise that we often looked like a team of individuals, each playing his own game, because that, in effect, was what we were. Under the tutelage of Sean Fallon and Jimmy McGrory, there were no tutorials in teamwork.

Players such as Bobby Lennox, Bobby Murdoch, wee Jinky and myself were breaking through as youngsters but we were clearly inexperienced and were playing against a lot of experienced players, so we would make mistakes. On one particular day, the crowd began giving Bob Kelly dog's abuse because of how poorly Celtic were playing. Afterwards, there was an obstreperous demonstration outside the main entrance to the ground. At that time, there was a medical television programme called *Your Life In Their Hands*. So, before the next match, Bob Kelly came into the dressing room and said, 'Do all you boys watch that programme *Your Life In Their Hands*? Well, today my life is in your hands.' Strangely enough, that little pep talk of his worked: we went out that day and turned it on. It was about then that we were nicknamed 'The Kelly Kids', since we were a group of youngsters breaking through together under the influence of the chairman.

Celtic were struggling when I first made my way into the team and Bob Kelly was on the end of fierce criticism from the supporters. He was constantly getting a really hard time – more so than the team on the park. Rangers were winning everything: in that 1963–64 season they won the treble, while we failed even to finish as runners-up to them in the League and were knocked out of both cup competitions by them in the early rounds. Rangers defeated us five times out of five that season and, in the fixtures between us, scored eleven goals to our one. They were a tremendous side and it wasn't a disgrace to be beaten by them, but it was galling for the supporters and us that Rangers got all the kudos and we won nothing. Supporters can only take so much of that sort of thing. But, while the fans gave Bob Kelly a hard time, they were quite kind to us because they saw that the side contained a lot of young players, and that we were starting to get better. Any flak that was going during a game, Bob Kelly got it and he got it heavily: 'Kelly Must Go' and all that sort of stuff – dog's abuse. I think the supporters did us a wee turn by getting on his back rather than ours.

Willie Henderson was almost always my direct opponent when we played against Rangers and between us, in the early 60s, I would say honours were even. He would get the ball at his feet and stick it past me, and he was greased lightning over 30 yards. I could catch him over 50 or 60 yards but he never went that far, only 20 or 30 yards. So I couldn't catch him because once he had knocked the ball past me I had to turn and chase him. He also had the advantage in that he always knew exactly what he was doing whilst I didn't know exactly what he was going to do, although I had a good idea. So by the time I had almost caught up with him, he would have crossed the ball for Jimmy Millar or Ralphie Brand. Around half the time he would get away from me in that fashion; the rest of the time I would tackle him hard before he was able to do his stuff. He would always know he had been in a game after he had played against me. After the first couple of times I had played against wee Willie, I knew exactly what to expect. Forewarned was forearmed.

Despite our domestic traumas, we managed to reach the semi-finals of the European Cup-Winners' Cup that 1963–64 season, which was quite a feat in what was only Celtic's second season of European football. When we won the first leg of our semi 3–0 against MTK Budapest at Celtic Park, we looked set for the final. The guys liked European football because you got two or three wee trips abroad and you saw places you wouldn't have seen in your life if you hadn't played football. That season in the European Cup-Winners' Cup we never seemed to get drawn against a club in a pleasant country such as France or Italy, always against communist countries – Yugoslavia, Czechoslovakia, Hungary. European football broke up the season and made an enjoyable change from domestic football, particularly as there was often an air of mystery about our opponents, whereas in Scotland we knew all about them. It wasn't always a delight: when you travelled to a communist country, you needed to go through the process of obtaining a visa and these places could often be grey and depressing. All the Iron Curtain countries at that time produced useful teams: the international teams of Czechoslovakia, the Soviet Union and Yugoslavia reached World Cup semi-finals and finals and European Nations Cup finals. So you didn't want to be drawn against them because they had great, skilful players. Also, the travel arrangements were often complicated and the standard of food and hotels poor.

At the time we faced MTK, Hungary was still trying to recover from the popular uprising against communism in 1956, when the Russian tanks had rolled into their country to restore the control of the Soviet Union. On travelling along the avenues of the city of Budapest, before playing our second leg there, we were impressed by the beautiful, magnificent buildings on the banks of the Danube – the architecture was superb. On all of these buildings, though, you could see the marks of shells and bullets and bits chipped out of the walls. It was actually quite frightening, and you shuddered to think what it had been like during the uprising. Yet, when we went to the Nep national stadium, where the match was to be played, the facilities were pristine and the pitch as smooth as the front lawn of a stately house. You would then go away from the stadium and do a bit of sightseeing and see that the people were going about in old, ragged jackets and jumpers with holes in them.

Over in Budapest, I played against a wee guy called Karoly Sandor, who had played in the great Hungarian national team of the '50s and '60s and was in his mid-thirties by that spring of

1964. Even at that age, what a going-over he gave me. I hadn't had any problems in the game at Celtic Park, principally because he had not played in the first leg, but he gave me a doing in Budapest. He was the trickiest type of outside-right, with a style similar to that of wee Jinky and nearly as good. I couldn't even catch him to kick him. I had a terrible game, but I was not our worst performer on the night; I don't think there was anyone in our team who played well in a match that saw us go down 4–0 and out of the Cup-Winners' Cup when we had been on the verge of our first European final. You would think that in a European semi, 3–0 up from the first leg, the management would tell us to keep things nice and tight and make the opposition chase the game and work for everything they were to get. No; Sean Fallon, who was in charge of team affairs by this time, wanted us to hump the ball 50 and 60 yards. You just don't do that sort of thing. We didn't deserve to get anything from the game, while they deserved to beat us 4–0 and maybe even by more.

The Hungarians were a totally different team to the one we had faced at Celtic Park. They had only made two changes to the team that had lined up against us in Glasgow but their attitude and approach to the match had altered radically. Even today, I still can't fathom why being at home or away in a European tie should affect players so much because you are still playing against the same guys, on the whole, in each match. It does count, though; it's a psychological thing. We had had the backing of a huge crowd at Celtic Park, which meant our tails were up in that game, and they had had the same in Budapest.

We finally found ourselves heading for an attractive European destination later in 1964, when we were drawn against Barcelona in the Fairs Cup. All of Europe had been awestruck by the Real Madrid side that had clinched a fifth successive European Cup win in 1960, and Barcelona, their major rivals, were almost as good a side. They beat us 3–1 over in the Nou Camp, which was full to the brim that night, and it was men against boys: as a team, they were in a different class. In the second leg at Celtic Park we played out of our skins to keep them to a 0–0 draw. Their right-back, Benitez, who was as strong as an ox, kept charging forwards, down on top of me, while I was trying to pick up their outside-right; it was the first time I had come across an overlapping full-back. We did well to keep them to that draw at Celtic Park. We were naïve: we didn't know how to change our game to play against European opposition, so we just went out and played as if we were playing a Scottish League game, which you don't do in Europe, especially against teams of that calibre. Still, we weren't winning any trophies at home so we could hardly be expected to be making a lot of progress in European competition.

Fortune may not have been going entirely the way of Celtic on the field of play but away from football I was making the most of being a professional footballer. I now had a Tony Curtis-style quiff and, when I was around seventeen, had started going to the dancing at the Trocadero in Hamilton, which eventually became wee Jimmy Johnstone's pub, The Double J. Each dance hall, such as the Trocadero, would have a mini-orchestra. The Dave Muir Band were resident at the Trocadero; they had eight or nine musicians and a female singer with a tremendous voice. They played all the big-band stuff and the dancing was waltzes, foxtrots and quicksteps; the only variation was the Twist, which was brand new in the early '60s. Other than that it was the normal, run-of-the-mill, one-two-three shuffle, one-two-three shuffle and so on. They were tremendous nights out: I would meet all the guys, such as my fellow apprentices from Ravenscraig, guys from the football teams in which I had played and guys with whom I had been at school. Most of those friends and acquaintances lived in the Motherwell, Wishaw, Hamilton, Uddingston, Bothwell and Carluke areas and the Troc was the place to go; the best ballroom in the area.

All the guys would be herded together on one side of the hall and all the women on the other, so you would have to make the long walk across the floor to ask a girl for a dance. 'Would you like to dance, darling?' If the answer was 'No, thank you' it felt like an even longer walk back, especially as all the boys would be having a great laugh at your expense. It happened to everybody so you couldn't get too uptight about it. I didn't have a car in those days so that left me struggling to get a bird at the end of the night; you could hardly get a bus ticket out of your pocket and say, 'I'll give you a run home.' Having your own transport was vital.

During the evening, if you got talking to a girl, they would find out from you, in a round about way, what means of transport you had. They'd ask, 'Where do you live?' I'd say, 'Craigneuk.' They'd say, 'How did you get here?' I'd have to respond, 'By bus,' and they would be finished with me; I would have no chance.

Entertainment for young people consisted of dancing or the movies. There were four picture halls and the Trocadero all in the one street in Hamilton, with another picture house further up the town. The main street in Motherwell had five cinemas and there was even a picture house in Craigneuk. Along with Tony Curtis, the stars who lit up the screen for me at the time were Bing Crosby, Sammy Davis, Frank Sinatra, Audrey Hepburn, Humphrey Bogart, Katharine Hepburn, Edward G. Robinson and Jimmy Cagney. The choice seemed pretty straightforward: a gangster movie, a romantic movie or a musical. That was it. Quite often you would see one of each within a week.

I had been quite reserved when I was a youngster, and I don't think I started to open up until I was fourteen or fifteen and had started playing football at school and then with Meadow Thistle and Coltness United. You get a bit of camaraderie with the boys in the team and it makes you open up; before that I wouldn't say boo to a goose. Then, when I signed for Celtic, I really became more confident and the press guys started calling me flamboyant. It could simply have been because the quiff in my ginger hair made me look a bit colourful. Anyway, once I read those words about myself I started trying to live up to them.

Once we had grown familiar with the rituals of 'the dancing' at the Troc and had grown out of that venue, we started going into Glasgow: to The Locarno in Sauchiehall Street, now The Garage nightclub; The Majestic; The Barrowland Ballroom; Dennistoun Palais, now a big supermarket; and Joanna's in Bath Street. The women in Lanarkshire were just as good-looking as those in Glasgow but the Lanarkshire women were a wee bit more sedate, more homely, more withdrawn, not as boisterous as the women in Glasgow, who were of a different breed. They could answer you back nice as ninepence; they had an answer for everything. They would call me a hick from the sticks for being from Craigneuk; they would be from places like Bridgeton and Barmulloch. Once you went into that Denny Palais or The Locarno or Barrowlands, you would be confronted by a host of 'gallus' women. They were right up for it, fancied themselves rotten and, if they could, they would take great pleasure in making a fool of you in front of their mates. There was no messing about with them: if they tried to hit you, they didn't miss you.

Initially, we would take the bus into Glasgow but once I started making a bit of money I could afford a car, and when I had a set of car keys to dangle, it made things a bit easier; in fact, it made it a different matter entirely. The car keys would be like a magnet to the girls and all you'd need to say would be 'Would you like a wee run home, darling?' With those magic words, you were in right away. Once I started playing regularly for Celtic, things became easier still. They knew for sure you had a motor, for starters, and that you must be getting decent money. You tried to fool yourself that they liked you for yourself but that was a delusion: it was because you had a car and played for Celtic.

I didn't drink much at that time: maybe two or three half-pints of lager before we went to the dancing and maybe a drink in the dancehall itself. None of us fell about the place; no one drank to excess. The dancing would start at about half past seven on a Saturday evening and finish fairly early, at about eleven o'clock, so that everybody could get the last bus home. It was pretty tame, civilised stuff. They could not finish later than eleven o'clock because otherwise all the folk would leave to get the bus and the place would be empty. Very few young people would be able to afford taxis.

As the mid-'60s arrived, I started to kick about the West End of Glasgow quite a bit; I felt I had outgrown Hamilton. I was starting to become a regular for Celtic and, although I was still living at home in Craigneuk with my parents, I would spend a lot of time in the city. I soon decided I was able to afford the cost of chipping in to rent a flat in Glasgow with three other guys for some fun nights. One of the other guys was John Cushley, a Celtic centre-half, who was doing an MA at Glasgow University, and the others were mates of mine who lived in Glasgow.

So we rented this flat in Clouston Street in the West End, just near the BBC building on Queen Margaret Drive and on the other side of the Botanic Gardens from Byres Road, but none of us lived there. You know what we were renting it for, don't you? The flat belonged to some arty people who had something to do with the theatre and were moving to London to run a theatre there. They didn't want to sell their place in Glasgow, so they rented it to us at a tenner a week. We had to let each other know when we were using it, because there were only three bedrooms. So if you picked up a bird you had to be quick – if you weren't fast you were last. We rented that house of fun for about a year. At the time we were going out with our future wives but this place was for our wee bits on the side.

The West End was jumping at that time – artistic types and beatniks were everywhere, there were loads of students about and the '60s were starting to swing. A lot of people came over to the West End from other areas, such as the south side, because the West End was like a magnet to people who were looking for a bit of sophistication and freedom. All the bars and the 'in' pubs, such as Curlers on Byres Road, were heaving. Once the pubs emptied at ten o'clock, we would go to the steakhouse, another buzzing centre of activity, and get stuck into these huge gammon steaks. We would pull a couple of birds and it was dead handy to get from Byres Road to Clouston Street. One of the girls with whom I had a bit of fun, and who shall remain nameless, later married one of my best pals. All that was when I was young and free and in my early twenties, so there was no damage done. It was mainly one-nighter jobs; none of that taking a girl out for a month and then giving her a kiss.

I enjoyed life to the full but I made sure I had my fun at the appropriate time: I wasn't out and about after a Wednesday, I never had a drink after a Wednesday night, and on Thursday and Friday nights I would be at home with my parents in Craigneuk, feet up, watching the telly and resting in advance of the match on the Saturday. After the game I would meet my mates in Glasgow, either at the Rogano or at an upmarket place in Gordon Street, opposite the Central Station, where they used cocktail shakers to mix your drinks and the bartenders had red jackets. It meant that we weren't running into the punters. It wouldn't have done for Celtic players to go down to the likes of Baird's Bar, would it?

We worked hard in training and matches and we played hard too. I was enjoying a way of life that would have been unimaginable if I had remained at Ravenscraig as an electrician. I would never have been able to afford a motor car or indulge in so many nights out. I had eventually ended my time at Ravenscraig in the summer of 1964, about three months before my apprenticeship was due for completion. I had told my foreman that once I had completed my apprenticeship I was going full-time with Celtic so they said that it was all right for me to leave early, and that, even though I was three months short of the five years necessary, I had served my apprenticeship. That was very generous of them, because it allowed me to go full-time in the summer of 1964 and get involved in pre-season training for the 1964–65 season.

I was still very much in the process of establishing myself in the first team, which at Celtic takes time. It was clear that the club's management left a lot to be desired, but I did not concern myself with that too much. Other players, though, who were established and had had several seasons at Celtic when there had been a lack of direction, were questioning whether their futures should lie at Celtic. Billy McNeill, for example, was becoming disillusioned about Rangers winning almost everything. He never discussed it with me but I knew that he could have gone to Tottenham Hotspur around 1964 or 1965 – he had been tapped by them – and that he was on the verge of agreeing to go south until he heard whispers that Jock Stein was returning to Celtic in early 1965. That offered all of us a bit of hope for the future. I had heard quite a lot about Jock from the likes of Billy McNeill, Paddy Crerand, Mike Jackson, John Divers and John Hughes, who had enjoyed working with him when he was in charge of the Celtic reserve team, and they all sang his praises. Those of us who had not worked with him had seen his Dunfermline Athletic side beat Celtic to win the Scottish Cup in 1961 and achieve some great results in Europe, such as defeating Valencia 6–2 at a time when Valencia were the Fairs Cup holders.

Life was sweet. I looked the part of the star footballer driving my first car, a Ford Zodiac, which was a great big, three-litre, six-cylinder job and a real gas-guzzler, styled a wee bit like the

American Chevy. I had bought it towards the end of my time at Ravenscraig, when I was just about to turn full-time at Celtic, so I was now driving back and forth between Celtic Park and Craigneuk. Every morning I would cut across to Chapelhall and pick up John Clark, then go past Viewpark and pick up wee Jinky and then on to Motherwell to collect Jimmy McGrory's secretary, a lassie called Anne McBride. We were all in our early twenties and living and loving life to the full but, as the news of Stein's imminent arrival at Celtic Park became more and more credible, we began to wonder if we might be about to be transported towards even greater adventures.

3. THE STEIN SCENE

Jock Stein was as fly as a barrel of monkeys and a great man to have on your side if his wiles were working in your favour. If he was working against you, then, as I eventually found out to my severe cost, things would almost certainly go badly for you. But that was the furthest thought from my mind when he took over as Celtic manager early in 1965. All I wanted to do was impress the man and show him how good a player I could be for him.

I knew big Jock liked attacking full-backs so, when I heard he was on his way to Celtic Park as manager, I started attacking in the hope that he would hear about it. I came in at half-time in the first match in which I tried to do that and Sean Fallon said, 'If you cross that halfway line again, son, you'll not be in the team.' So it was back to making 60-yard passes. Sean was very enthusiastic when he was in charge of the team, but he had played in an era where it was all about humping the ball from back to front, so I think he just carried on with the basic tactics prevalent in his day without realising that the game was starting to change a bit and that people were thinking more about the game and the way in which it was played.

Jimmy McGrory had by the mid-'60s taken a back seat and Sean was doing almost all the running of the team but we hadn't learned anything that was new or would help us. I think Bob Kelly had realised that we were standing still and decided that he would need to make changes. I don't know this for a fact, but I would assume that when big Jock was asked to come back he would have wanted to sort out his own backroom team. Bob Kelly, however, asked him if he would have Sean as his assistant. I think the deal might have been that Stein was to be team boss as long as he kept Sean on as his assistant, because Sean and Bob Kelly were very friendly, shall we say. Sean had always made sure that whatever Bob Kelly asked to be done was done. Bob Kelly would be making the bullets in the background and Sean would fire them. If Bob Kelly wanted to know what was going on in the dressing room, he would have Sean reporting back everything he had heard.

Once big Jock arrived, the club was turned upside down. He said he wanted me to charge forward down the touchline, so I was now being asked to do the opposite of what I had been told to do by Sean. Big Jock's first game was against Airdrie at Broomfield in early March 1965; we won 6–0, wee Bertie scored five, and from kick-off I was charging down that left-hand side like nobody's business. I went in at half-time and Jock said, 'Listen, son, I know you like to go forward but you go forward when the time is right. You don't go forward all the time. Remember, first and foremost you are a defender. You should go forward if the opportunity is there, but you are just going forward willy-nilly, even when it is not on.' With Sean Fallon it had been a case of hump it up the park as quickly as possible but with Jock Stein the trick was to go forward at the right time and defend at the right time. I played it by ear and we also worked on it a lot in training, creating the circumstances for going on the overlap or refraining from doing so. So when I got into a match situation, I would know when was the right time to go and when to stay.

Things quickly fell into place under Jock. Training methods changed; we started to get balls to practise with, which we had very seldom had before. Big Jock changed almost everything. The days of the 60-yard pass were just about over. He started us playing from the back, through the midfield to the front players. The first person I was to look for, whenever I had won the ball, was Bertie Auld, and he would never be more than 25 yards away from me. On occasion, I could still use a long pass, if, for example, I could see Bobby Lennox was one-on-one with a defender, because Bobby, with his pace, would always leave an opponent standing. If you had time to play with the ball, he wanted you to knock it around and build the game up, although if you were under pressure at the back, his orders were to get rid of the ball into the stand; nobody has scored from the stand yet. Jock made us play for each other; we had never been coached in how to do that. I think everybody had a lot to prove to big Jock, to show that they were good enough to play for him, and that helped him to have an immediate effect on confidence, ability and teamwork. He always hammered into us that football is a team game but one in which you need a little individuality now and again – we had some great individuals. He gave us a sense of purpose.

Jock Stein totally transformed the club in two months and we reached the 1965 Scottish Cup final, where we would meet Dunfermline Athletic on 24 April. He had experimented with the team during the matches in March and early April because the 1964–65 League title was already lost by then – in fact, we would finish eighth in the League that season. So being in the team for the final of the Scottish Cup was the target for everyone. I was left out for a couple of games and Jim Kennedy took my place, then I came back into the team but was again left out of the side for the home match with Partick Thistle, the final League match of the season, on the Saturday before the final with Dunfermline. So I was wondering where I stood; I didn't know if I'd a chance of playing in the final because Jock always kept his cards close to his chest. You couldn't jump to conclusions. He would tell us what he wanted to tell us and nothing else. Before that final, I think he was keeping us all on tenterhooks about whether we would be playing or not. Everyone was desperate to play in that game: we were all on a high because we had a new manager, new tactics, a new system and new training methods.

He told us the team on the Friday morning. I was relieved to find out that I was playing. We knew we were going to have a hard time from Dunfermline, who at that time had a very good side, and we did find it challenging that afternoon. I was playing against wee Alec Edwards, who was still only a teenager. He was a very good player and gave me a bit of trouble but I think, over the piece, I was all right and played a reasonable game. We were a goal behind twice, equalised twice, through Bertie both times, and then, nine minutes from the end, Billy McNeill knocked in the header that won the game for us. I think we deserved it: we had played better as a side, and with more commitment. I think we were hungrier than Dunfermline in wanting to win it, and it was Jock Stein who had created that hunger. Winning that final was a transformation in itself because previously we had kept getting to semi-finals or finals and losing them. Now we had won a final at Stein's first attempt and everything just snowballed from there.

Once you start winning matches, confidence builds; an average player becomes a good one, and a good player a great one. Jock's cleverness lay in recognising individual abilities and piecing the whole thing together. He asked everyone to play to their strengths and never asked them to do anything they couldn't do. If you tried to do something else, then you got a bollocking. He bonded eleven players into a team and made us realise that, although we were playing different roles, we all depended on each other. It sounds so simple – but that simplicity was the key to everything.

We now had a totally refreshed club with an entirely different atmosphere. All of a sudden, you saw a wee bit of light at the end of the tunnel; you could see that Stein had brought more professionalism to the place. The training regime was overhauled so that it was now serious; you would still have a bit of fun and hilarity, because you always get that, but things were mostly done in a purposeful, businesslike manner.

We soon had the teamwork down to a tee. We knew, when we were out there playing, that if somebody was having a bad game or being given a difficult time, the rest of us would get around and help them. We would have arguments during matches but at the end of the game, if we had won, we would accept that it had been for the general good because it had worked. We would also have altercations in training. We had a twenty-minute game at the end of each session, which everyone would take quite seriously, and two or three times a week there would be punch-ups among the players, but at the end everyone would shake hands and we would all start with a clean slate the following day. That was good: it told you that there was a bit of spirit about the place and that everybody wanted to be a winner. If you get kicked you have to show a bit of animosity or retaliate. Big Jock liked to see that and he would also pick out opposition players of whom he would say, 'If you get in about him he will disappear from the game.'

There were players I played against whom, if you growled at them, you would never see in the game again. Jim McLean, who later became manager of Dundee United, was a very skilful attacking player for Kilmarnock and Dundee, a good user of the ball, someone who could pass the ball 60 yards and make sure it landed at a team-mate's feet, but I knew that, if I hit him hard and early, he would be give me a quiet afternoon. As a defender you could always try to intimidate front players because there weren't too many of them who had the heart of a lion. Some were tough. You could hit wee Willie Henderson as often as you wanted to but he would still bounce back. Jinky was the same, as was Willie Johnston, another Rangers winger. I played against him on the right side and the left side and he kept coming back for more. George Best, too: you couldn't intimidate him. I played against him in a couple of friendlies for Celtic against Manchester United and also for Scotland against Northern Ireland. You knew that if you could not intimidate a winger, you were in for a harder game than normal, so that separated the men from the boys.

Jock was a disciplinarian when he had to be: when he had to put his foot down, he didn't mess about. You knew what you could get away with, without stretching it. If I tried to be too clever in training and started taking players on, he would whistle and say, 'Hey you, cut it out. You can't do that.' He could make you feel about an inch tall, just with one sentence, so you made sure you did as he wished. Wee Jinky was terrified of him. Jock used to get hold of him and wee Bobby Lennox by the scruff of the neck – although he wasn't going to hit them or anything – and tell them to stop messing about. We all respected him. You've got to respect somebody who makes you better at your job, and that's what he did. You didn't mess about when Jock was trying to get something across in training, such as different tactics; it was serious stuff. He was very strict about that: you never messed about in your preparations for match days. If you tried to, he would have a quiet word in your ear or he would leave you out of the team – and at that time you needed to be in the team to get your bonuses to pay the mortgage and for your spending money.

I remember big Jock saying to me that when he had been playing for Celtic in the '50s, with Jimmy McGrory as manager, the players had tried to sort out a few tactical things among themselves, such as picking up ball players and getting on top of the man who made the opposition team tick. Now that he was manager, he had defenders going forward, midfield players linking up with full-backs, and wingers going infield to leave space on the touchline for full-backs to overlap. Bobby Lennox would go inside to leave space for me to overlap and Jimmy Johnstone would do the same for Jim Craig on the other flank. These were all things that came from big Jock when he arrived at Celtic. He had been to Inter Milan with Willie Waddell to study the methods of Helenio Herrera, the Inter manager. Jock learned a lot there, tactically, and came back with many good ideas. Herrera was the master at that time and his Inter side had won the European Cup in 1964 and 1965 with Giacinto Facchetti, the Inter left-back, as the premier overlapping full-back in Europe. Big Jock took that into account and that was how I started doing what I was doing.

I think it shows you the true value of Bob Kelly that he brought Jock back as manager. He probably had to swallow a lot of pride to make that decision but it was made easier for him by the heavy criticism he had been getting from the supporters. Big Jock told me that, when he first went back, Bob Kelly would try to interfere with team selections in the same way that he had screened Jimmy McGrory's teams. They would still have their board meetings on a Thursday night and big Jock would know what his team was going to be. Bob Kelly would say, 'What's your team for Saturday?' and Jock would respond, 'Mr Kelly, you brought me back as team manager, in charge of team selection, and I don't want any interference from you whatsoever.' Bob Kelly tried several times to impose his will on team selection but, once it was established that Jock was in sole control of team affairs and the team began winning regularly, there was no hassle whatsoever. Another thing happened when big Jock came back: the anti-Protestant bigotry of a small minority of players disappeared. With a Protestant manager, they couldn't very well say anything about Proddy players, could they?

Old Firm matches now began to swing our way, and much of that was down to Jock. It must have been hard for Willie Henderson to play against me because Rangers were still in the dark ages at that time, playing the system we ourselves had used before Jock had arrived, in which the wingers' job was to get down the line and fire the ball across for the centre-forward. So big Jock said to me, 'Stand on Henderson's right-hand side and let him come across you because he will do nothing on his left-hand side – he will just go across the park – but if you let him go down the touchline you will get problems.' Willie was right-footed and I could use my left or right so I had the advantage over him if he was forced on to his left side and infield.

So I just about stood on wee Willie's right boot, on the touchline, and made him come inside and kept him moving across the park. He would go across the park from one touchline to the other and wouldn't know what to do with the ball, as his game at that time was based on going outside the full-back, hitting the goal-line and crossing. With me blocking him on the outside he was completely lost. That's an example of Jock making sure I played to my strengths and disguised my weaknesses. It's difficult for defenders to catch fast wingers when you've got to turn and chase them, so we had to try something else, and that's what we tried with wee Willie. It worked.

At that time, Rangers would play John Greig at left-back against us to thump wee Jimmy. In one game, in the first five minutes, Greig went right through Jimmy and sent him off the park and on to the running track. At that time, the referee would give an offending player a finger-wigging so that he knew he couldn't do it again. So as soon as Jimmy was sent on to the track by Greig, I went right up behind Willie and said, 'Hey, wee man, you're getting the same as Greig has just dished out to wee Jinky.' He turned and looked at me, alarmed. 'What have I done to you?' Willie is a good friend of mine – we still keep in touch – and he will tell you that he was never injured playing against me. I would trip him, tug his jersey, obstruct him – things that don't hurt– but I never went over the ball to try to break his leg or anything like that. It might have been easier on our side if I *had* gone over the top of the ball and done his ankle or his knee but I never kicked anybody unless they kicked me first, and he never did. There were a few players in that Rangers team, though, who would think nothing of going over the top of the ball and breaking your leg.

Jock got the best out of me in Old Firm games, and out of Jinky too. If Jimmy was kicked on to the running track by a defender, we were told to take a short free kick quickly and give the ball back to him. He could then run at the same defender again, because the other player, having only just given away a free kick, could not touch Jimmy again or he would be on a booking. So that was a wee bit of intimidation in reverse, on Jock's instructions. It worked all the time. The defender would have been told to stop Jinky at all costs as early in the game as possible and that was the way we got round it.

Rangers had made the biggest bloomer of the lot when they sold Jim Baxter to Sunderland: he was a magnificent player on the ball and the guy that made them tick. I don't think I ever saw him waste a pass and his confidence was immense. The two things that really turned the tide in our favour were big Jock coming back and giving us the low down on the tactical side of things and Baxter leaving Rangers in the summer of 1965.

After Celtic v Rangers games, three or four players from each side would meet up in Reid's Bar in Hope Street, which is now Bar Cini. Reid's Bar belonged to Tam Reid, chairman of Partick Thistle and SFA President, and then to Miller Reid, Thistle chairman. One of its principal attractions was this big, buxom barmaid; Willie Henderson knew her well. They had a wee private bar up above the busy main premises, so after the game Willie would fix it up with this barmaid to have the bar ready for the boys coming in at half-five or so. She'd be working there and we'd get a bit of privacy. We might have been punching and kicking each other during the game, but once we got in there, had a few beers, talked about the game briefly, talked about something else, such as European trips or birds, things would be pretty mellow. You would have Rangers players such as wee Willie, Ronnie McKinnon, Davie Provan and Willie Johnston mixing with myself, Willie Wallace and Bertie Auld. The fans would never have believed this was going on. Half of them called me a bastard and the other half cheered me but both sets would probably have been displeased to know that Celtic and Rangers players were fraternising so soon after a match.

With Jock at the helm, we also began to make progress in European football and, in his first full season at Celtic, 1965–66, we reached the quarter-finals of the European Cup-Winners' Cup, in which we defeated Dynamo Kiev 3–0 in the first leg of the tie at Celtic Park on 12 January. For the return, Dynamo Kiev chose to switch the match to Tbilisi, down close to the Turkish border, because Kiev in January was under several feet of snow. We took over great big hampers of food: steaks, chickens and so on. Jimmy Steele, our physio, was also in charge of grub so for our pre-match meal in Tbilisi he said we would all be getting half a chicken each: Marshall's chunky chicks, he said, which were really popular. We were looking forward to them. When the meal arrived, we were expected to feast on the skinniest, scrawniest of chickens. The hotel's kitchen staff had kept all the Marshall's chunky chicks and had given us local chickens with these long, spindly legs. Steelie got some stick for that.

The return match ended 1–1. 'Big Yogi' – John Hughes – knocked the ball back for me to hit a screamer of a goal for us. So that was us in the semi-finals and we had a magnificent party after the game in one of the hotel rooms. We made sure the three stewardesses from the plane were with us to help the celebrations swing. We had discovered this pink champagne, magnificent stuff, and were simply sticking it on the room bill. We gave the waiter a ten-bob note – a fortune in the Soviet Union at that time – and he came to us every half an hour with half a dozen bottles of this pink champagne. All this was still going on at three o'clock in the morning when the captain of our Aer Lingus plane chapped the door of the room, bevvied. We were supposed to be flying out from Tbilisi with this captain as our pilot, at half past eight that morning, yet here he was looking for some of our supplies. Wee Bertie handed him a half-full bottle of Black Label and told him to finish it off.

We players were pretty fit so although, in the morning, we had hangovers, we could handle them. It was different for the pilot. Aer Lingus told us there was a technical fault with the plane but it was more that there was one with the pilot: they couldn't get him sobered up. We had all been at the airport bang on the button, awaiting the crew. The stewardesses and steward were there on time too, but the two pilots were missing. You could see the steam coming out of Jock's ears. We didn't take off until about five hours later and went from Tbilisi to Moscow where we found the city blanketed by about three feet of snow. That stop in Moscow was, I think, the one and only time I saw Desmond White, the club secretary, handing out money freely. He had bundles of roubles and he was peeling off wads of notes and handing them out because there was no point in taking them back to Scotland: outside the Soviet Union they were worthless. There wasn't much to buy at Moscow Airport, but quite a few of us acquired Russian cameras.

From there we were supposed to fly to Copenhagen to refuel but that airport was closed so they diverted us to Stockholm, where the aeroplane's wings kept freezing up. We were on the plane, with the wings de-iced and ready for take-off, three times, but the flaps would quickly become iced up again. Finally Bob Kelly said, 'No way are we getting on that plane tonight.' He may have had in his mind thoughts of the 1958 Munich Disaster, when a plane carrying the Manchester United team had crashed on attempting to take off on a similarly icy day. We had a match with Hearts, in Edinburgh, scheduled for Saturday afternoon but we would now have to spend Thursday night in Sweden.

The club put us into the Grand Hotel in Stockholm – quite a place, with an orchestra whose musicians all wore the nattiest of white dinner suits, as did the wealthy male guests, who, with their wives, looked like counts and countesses, while we were going around in our tracksuits and training shoes. On the following day we had the same problem of the flaps icing up. So, rather than have us sit around in the hotel all day, the club put us all in a coach and took us away out into the countryside to a lovely restaurant beside a large, frozen lake. We eventually took off from Stockholm late that evening and got into Prestwick after midnight. I had brought back cigarettes for my mother and father, and when the customs man at Prestwick searched my bags he found I had 200 over the limit, but he did not make a note of the camera I had bought at Moscow Airport. So he pointed out a desk and told me to go there and pay the duty on the extra cigarettes. Jimmy Farrell, the director, who was standing there, blurted out, 'Oh, did you get caught with the camera you bought in Russia as well?' I said, 'No, Mr Farrell, I don't have a camera. I've got extra cigarettes on which I've got to pay duty.' Luckily, the customs man turned a deaf ear to our little exchange.

By now, we were in the early hours of Saturday, with a League game to play later that afternoon. From the airport in Ayrshire Jock took us straight to Celtic Park, where we put our training gear on and played a nine-a-side match on the pitch at half past one in the morning. It was close to four o'clock by the time I got home to Motherwell and I had to be back at Celtic Park at ten. We went to Tynecastle that day absolutely shattered and Hearts beat us 3–2, with Willie Wallace scoring twice for them. I'm not taking anything away from Willie but we were in no fit state to play a football match. You could see, after half an hour, that all the boys were the same: there was no sharpness about us at all. That was the worst trip we had in all the years we were in Europe, although it was also a hugely memorable one. It was also, not surprisingly, the last time we flew with Aer Lingus.

Jock was a teetotaller but I don't think he had a problem with players having a drink. He never drank when he played, but players around about him in the '50s, such as Charlie Tully and John McPhail, certainly did like a drink. So he couldn't have a hang-up about it. Seamill Hydro, on the Ayrshire coast, was where the Celtic squad would go whenever he wanted to keep us all together, and our base before we played in Cup finals or European ties at Celtic Park. Sometimes he would take us down to Seamill from Monday to Wednesday to give us different surroundings for training. The Hydro had a lot of elderly residents who stayed there all the year round, as if it were their retirement home, and we got to know them well. There were about a dozen of them, all smashing people; we were on first-name terms with them and they loved us. So Jock would tell us in the evening that we could have a couple of drinks but we must not drink in the Hydro, because he didn't want these old folk to see us drinking. He was very careful of the club's image and always did all he could to make sure that we didn't tarnish our own images in any way.

So he would let us out from the Hydro for a couple of drinks but he would have a curfew. Big Jock would sit at the door of the Hydro with Neilly Mochan, Sean Fallon, Bob Rooney and Jimmy Steele and they would all play solo. Big Jock only needed four hours of sleep a night so he never wanted to go to bed early. That meant that all the members of the backroom team had to stay up with him. Neilly would check all the rooms at curfew time and if we weren't in them he had to tell big Jock. The next morning, if you had strayed from his instructions, he would take you down to the beach and murder you at training. If anything really outrageous happened he would fine you a tenner. Occasionally after matches in Europe we would throw pints at each other and splash the walls of the hotel, the club would be charged for repairs and what not and Jock would fine us a tenner each to pay for the damage. We always seemed to draw these Iron Curtain countries and there was nothing you could do there – you couldn't even spend your money. So all you could do was drink pints and, of course, you get fed up drinking pints, so, being the tearaways that we once were, we would start throwing them at each other.

We were clever, though, in that we did all those things behind closed doors so we never got caught. The press guys who were with us were all football reporters, not news reporters, so if there were a few misdemeanours we would ask them to turn a blind eye. Then we would give them a wee story about something the following week.

One of Jock's quirks was that he would come up to a front player on a Thursday morning at training and tell him that he had been doing well in previous games. You could then be sure that, for the following game, that player would be dropped. We picked up on that pretty quickly. Bobby Lennox and wee Jinky would always be in the forward line but he would alternate between John Hughes, Willie Wallace, Joe McBride and Stevie Chalmers and, if he spoke to one of them on the Thursday morning, you would know that that player would be absent from the team on Saturday. We used to talk about it in the bath after training almost every Thursday: 'Right, who did he speak to this morning?' I think he knew that we knew that was the way he worked. Maybe he did it to soften the blow of being dropped. The players would then be entitled to say, 'You told me I was playing brilliantly and then you left me out?' And he'd say something like: 'I just thought it needed changing a wee bit and that we needed big Yogi's power up front instead of your guile.' He was fantastic at flannelling, a master at taking the heat off himself. But he always seemed to have a plausible reason for whatever he had done. You believed him at the time, then you would go away and say to yourself, 'That was a load of shit he was talking back there' – but by then there was nothing you could do about it.

Supporters held him in awe, partly because of what he had done before he came to Celtic and partly because he achieved results quickly and consistently right from the start of his time as the manager. I don't think 'awe' would be the word that we players would use, though, to describe how we felt about him. We respected him highly and, although we weren't terrified of him or anything like that, we knew that if he said something you had to do it.

He was a man determined to control every aspect of a situation. In a room, he had to get the seat facing the door, so that he could see everything that was happening. Whether it was Seamill Hydro or a restaurant, he would sit where he could see everybody who was going out and coming in, everybody who was going to the bar and what everybody was drinking. We would ask him if we could have a couple of pints and he would say, 'Fine, but no more than a couple of pints.' So we would have a couple of pints and then go up to our rooms, where we would get to work on a carry-out that we would have brought with us. What he didn't see didn't hurt him.

He still caught us a few times; it didn't matter which hotel we were in, he always had the pass-key for everybody's room. He would tell us to go to our beds, so we would go up to our rooms, get out a half-bottle of vodka plus a few lagers and invite somebody in from next door to come and join us. So we would be sitting there scooping up the drinks when suddenly we would hear the pass-key turning in the door and big Jock would come in, raging, tell us to get to our beds and pour the booze down the sink. That was his favourite trick and I lost count of the number of hotels it happened in, both abroad and at the Seamill Hydro or the Marine Hotel in Troon. He always seemed to know when we were boozing. He would watch someone go upstairs at ten o'clock, for example, and realise that he was going to bed unusually early and work out that he was up to something.

At Seamill Hydro, there was a chandelier above where Jock and the backroom boys used to sit. He made sure we were all billeted on the first floor so that he could check everything on the one floor – but also, every time someone began moving about on that floor, the chandelier rattled above the reception area where he would be playing solo with Neilly and the others. Immediately, Neilly or Bob Rooney would be sent up to check the rooms. I think he probably caught every player in the club at one time or another doing something they shouldn't have been doing, simply by using his pass-key.

Sometimes, we would be away in a hotel and he would have ordered us not to take any drink. So we would be sitting there with glasses of Coca-Cola. Now, Jock knew which of the boys liked a drink more than the others, so he would go up to one of them and say, 'Here, I'm dead thirsty. Can I have a wee mouthful of your Coke?' – to find out if there was any vodka or whisky or Bacardi in it. He was very clever – he made it look as if it was quite natural, not as if he was checking up on us so that when he did find something untoward he could appear even more offended. But there were also a lot of times when he didn't catch us; when he would use the pass-key and we would be sitting there reading in our beds. We wouldn't break the rules when there was a big match on the horizon; it would only be when we were down there for a two- or three-day break without a game that we would get a wee carry-out for a nightcap.

When we were all younger, before we got into the marriage stakes, we would go on trips and look to find a few birds. Like any bunch of young guys, if we got a chance to go looking for a bird, we would take it. We all had our moments. Jock would quickly sense if something like that was going on and he would always get Neilly to check it out. Neilly would tell the player to finish it and then he would go back to big Jock and tell him that nothing was happening. They worked well as a team: Neilly took the heat out of a lot of things and prevented situations from resulting in a head-to-head with the big man.

On his arrival at Celtic Park, Jock had changed the training schedules. We had never, under the Jimmy McGrory regime, been given any shooting practice worth talking about: corner kicks or free kicks or dead-ball situations. Jock introduced that and a handful of us got the chance to practise shooting from 25 yards: myself, along with Bobby Murdoch, Joe McBride and Charlie

Gallagher. He got to know who could do it and sorted the tactics out accordingly. When there was a free kick from 20 or 25 yards out, Bertie was to knock it to the side to me to hit the ball. I was pleasantly surprised to find how well and how powerfully I could hit the ball and it got me into the scoring habit. Rodger Baillie, who worked for the *Daily Record*, came along to Barrowfield one day with a radar device and used it to time the shots hit by one player from every team in Scotland's top division. I won the competition after my shot was timed at 71 miles per hour.

Before games, and down at Seamill, Big Jock used to give Jimmy Steele a hand to give us a rub-down and all that sort of stuff; anything that needed to be done, Jock would muck in with it. We would have a collective team talk just before we went out for a match and then he would go to each player individually and check that they knew exactly what their job was to be. He was good at getting the team spirit going before we went out. He was always very confident on match days in the dressing room and that was to help us, to give us a bit of confidence as well. He did it well and didn't sound as if he was flanelling. Once he was in the dugout he let himself be heard, especially by referees and linesmen. He didn't miss them. If I was trying to be too clever or not doing what I was supposed to be doing, he would get word to me all right, even if I was on the far side of the park. He was very clever at reading a game: he could see things happening more quickly than most people and was quick at putting them right if necessary. He never went crazy on the touchline; he would shout and give directions but he wouldn't be leaping six feet in the air.

We just got better and better and better. During the 1965–66 season I played in all 60 matches in all four competitions and it was great to win the League Championship at Fir Park, clinching the club's first title in twelve years. It was a nice wee twist of fate for me, the boyhood Motherwell supporter, to win it there. By then, though, I was very much a Celtic man; I had long ago metamorphosed from being the kid with aspirations to play for the 'Well. They made it hard for us that day. I remember well that there were folk up on top of the roof of the stand who couldn't get into the ground. They saw us win 1–0, which meant that we won the League by finishing two points clear of Rangers.

Disappointingly, however, we lost to Rangers in the Scottish Cup final. We thought we had done enough to win but we drew the first match 0–0. In the replay on the Wednesday night we lost a poor goal from a defensive point of view, because Big Yogi had not come back to pick up Kai Johansen, which allowed him a free shot and he scored from about 25 yards. I also think Ronnie Simpson was blinded at the goal; there were a few players in front of him. That was the only goal of the match and it prevented us securing the first treble in Celtic's history as we had beaten Rangers earlier in the season in the final of the League Cup. I don't remember an awful lot else about that Scottish Cup final; I find that when you lose a big match like that, you tend to put it out of your mind.

Through defeating Dynamo Kiev we had reached the semi-finals of the European Cup-Winners' Cup for the second time in three years. In the semi we gave Liverpool, who were England's champions-elect, a real going-over in the first leg at Celtic Park but beat them by only 1–0. We hit the crossbar two or three times, hit the post, had two or three cleared off the line. The score really did flatter Liverpool: we should have been 3–0 or 4–0 up after that first leg. Down at Anfield in the second leg, they were 2–0 up when Bobby Lennox scored a valid goal only for it to be ruled offside; they show it on television now and again and Bobby is clearly onside when he collects the ball. That was a big disappointment but maybe it was the right thing to happen to us in that it may have geed us up for the following year, when we were in the European Cup for the first time. It is possible that the disappointment of losing the Liverpool game made us determined not to experience that feeling again. If we had got past Liverpool and had beaten Borussia Dortmund in the final, which, in 1966, was at Hampden Park, we might not have had the same hunger for the European Cup the following year.

Everywhere we went during that 1965–66 season, there were full houses. Before matches, in the dressing room, we would say to each other, 'What will it be today, boys? Two, three or four to us?' That's how confident we were in our own ability, as a team and as individuals. The only question was whether we could get even better in the 1966–67 season.

4. OUR GREATEST GOAL

We entertained no thoughts of winning the European Cup as we delved into that tournament for the first time in the autumn of 1966 with a match against FC Zurich of Switzerland. We had had a reasonable run in Europe the previous season and were hoping to get a similar run in the 1966–67 season; that was all we wanted and expected. We just wanted some more of the fun that European games offered because those games were always special: we had to adjust to opponents with a different approach, and pitting our wits against the Europeans was a challenge we always enjoyed.

Zurich was a good draw for us: on paper it looked OK, and that was how it worked out on the field of play. We beat them home and away and I scored three goals in the two legs as we won on a 5–0 aggregate. I scored two identical goals in the tie. In the first leg I was about 30 yards from goal when I struck the ball high into the Zurich net to score Celtic's first goal in the European Cup. In Switzerland I was again 30 yards from goal on the same side of the park when I hit the ball from almost exactly the same spot and angle as in the first leg. You would have thought the goalkeeper would have learned from the first one at Celtic Park but obviously he did not. My other strike was a penalty. The aggregate score suggests it was an easy tie but there is nothing easy until you are in front. We probably thought we should have scored more than two goals at Celtic Park but as soon as we scored over there, it was all over. I was surprised that they didn't put more into the game and make life difficult for us. You got the impression, after we had scored the first goal over there, that they had had enough.

Ladislav Kubala, the great Hungarian who had been at Barcelona, was by then Zurich's player–coach and played in midfield against us in the second leg. He was built like an ox and could still play a bit, even though he was 39.

We had stayed in a hotel in Switzerland called the Dolder Grand; what you might call a seven-star job. Big Jock let us go out for a wee stroll so we went into a local café and ordered some Coca-Colas, which, in 1966, cost us £5 each, so we didn't order any more. Those trips to Europe broke up the season nicely. I had never been in a hotel in my life until I had gone to Dublin to play for the Scottish Junior side in the early '60s, so seeing all these hotels in Europe, with their exquisite furnishings and fabulously wealthy people milling around, was a real eye-opener for me.

One of Jimmy Steele's many tasks was to keep things right with the kitchen when we went on European trips. We never got foods covered in rich sauces, just steak, chicken and fish – the very best of stuff but nothing fancy. Jock wouldn't allow us to use any hotel swimming pools – he said that swimming weakened your muscles – and we wouldn't be allowed out in the sun. It was all very controlled, although, after a game, Jock would let us off the leash to have a few drinks, unless we had put on a terrible display, which didn't happen too often. Sometimes, if we were returning from a midweek match in Europe on a Thursday afternoon, Jock would take us straight from the airport to Celtic Park for a training session.

We had started using a 4–2–4 system with two wide men in that 1966–67 season. Jinky would more or less always be on the right and it varied on the left between Bobby Lennox and big Yogi. When we got the ball on the left, Yogi or Bobby would make a run to take the right-back away and that would leave a huge gap into which I could run. That would be the signal for me to go. I would only make an overlap when Bertie Auld or Bobby Murdoch had the ball and then it was up to whoever was on the left-hand side in front of me to make a run and take his marker away, leaving me with the freedom of the park on the left-hand side. We would use the surprise element a lot: Bobby Murdoch or Bertie would fiddle around in the middle of the park, then signal to Bobby Lennox or Yogi to make a run inside, taking the right-back with them, and I would then make a run up the wing, latch on to the ball and move forward. At that time, the opposition would rarely be up to speed with big Jock's tactics so I would find that when I went forward, nobody would challenge me. By the time my opponent, the outside-right, had spotted what I had done, I would be away from him and, even if he chased after me, he would rarely be able to catch me.

We had played a 2–3–5 system against Dunfermline in the 1965 Scottish Cup final and throughout the 1965–66 season; Jock did not change the system to 4–2–4 until we went to Bermuda, Canada and the United States for an eleven-game post-season tour after the 1966 Scottish Cup final. That summer of 1966, over in North America, wee Bertie was transformed from being a left-winger into a left-sided midfield player, which would be vital for us because there were few better at putting piercing passes through a defence. That tour also really bound us together as a team – a team of pals – because we were away from home for nearly six weeks. A lot of good friendships were forged during that time and the repartee between the guys was brilliant. Everybody got on so well together. We didn't have any cliques: everybody mixed in and we all performed wee wind-ups on each other. We were also all from roughly the same background so we understood each other very well. Some players were more serious-minded than others, such as Billy McNeill, Jim Craig, John Clark and Stevie Chalmers. The more serious players were, on the whole, those who had been through the bad old days before we younger ones started to come through. I think they thought that they had better not take too much for granted even though things had taken a turn for the better under Jock Stein. Stevie has always been on the quieter side. Billy isn't but John Clark is: you've got to squeeze information out of John. Billy would never shut up on the park: he was always moaning at you or cajoling you, giving you stick. We were entitled to do the same thing back to him, though, if we felt he could be doing better for the team.

Bertie teamed up in midfield with Bobby Murdoch, who had been moved to the right side of midfield almost from the moment Jock arrived at Celtic Park; before that he had been playing in the forward line. So our new 4–2–4 formation featured Bobby and

Bertie spraying passes here and there for four pacy forwards and for the two overlapping full-backs. Bobby and Bertie could also score goals themselves. Many attacking opportunities were now available to us, and attacking moves could develop from almost every point on the park.

In central defence, Billy was brilliant in the air but wasn't the quickest on the deck so John Clark and Billy were a perfect foil for each other. Anything that went past Billy on the deck, John swept up and gave it to somebody. John couldn't beat many people in the air but he didn't need to do so because Billy won everything that came into the heart of our defence over head-height.

All the other sides in Scotland had stood still: they were still playing variations on the old 2–3–5 formation. So that put us a step ahead of them right away. Before they had realised what had hit them we would be a couple of goals up. They didn't know how to mark the players in our system because they were used to the old-fashioned WM formation. Big Jock was always a thinker about the game: he could go and see a team play, analyse them perfectly and come back and tell you their strengths and weaknesses. Most of the time, though, he didn't bother outlining too much of it because he knew that if we played to our strengths we would do the business anyway. It was when we didn't play to our strengths that we were in trouble.

Our second trip abroad in the European Cup was to play Nantes, the champions of France, in the second round. Their pitch was the widest I have ever played on. They really stretched the distance from the edge of the box to the touchline. Celtic Park is pretty wide but you could add another ten yards to that. It is amazing the difference it makes to be playing on a wide pitch like that. Nantes had a couple of wingers and it suited them: the more space the front players have, the easier it is for them to play. As it turned out, it didn't make much difference because the game was a stroll in the park for us. By that stage in the season we were playing exceptionally well. Continental clubs do not expect to be put under pressure at home in European ties; they expect to run the show and for the away team to defend. We were of the belief that we could play only one way and that that was to attack – so that surprised them. We won 6–2 on aggregate – 3–1 in each leg – and they were pretty straightforward matches. Nobody could touch us at home or abroad: before the first leg with Nantes in November 1966 we had scored 45 goals in only twelve Scottish League matches and had captured the League Cup by beating Rangers in the final for a second successive season.

Once you got through one round of the European Cup, you couldn't wait for the draw to see whom you were getting in the next round. When we heard that Vojvodina Novi Sad were to be our opponents in the quarter-final it made for a bit of mystery because we did not know a great deal about them. Our first reaction was: 'Where is that?' Again, we thought we had a good draw, because we had avoided Inter Milan and Real Madrid.

Novi Sad was a dump of a town. Poverty was its public face; there were no large, fancy buildings or cathedrals adorning its streets. The stadium wasn't a fancy place either: it was pretty modest, about the same size as Motherwell's ground with terracings wide open to the elements. The crowd were wrapped up in their winter mufflers and heavy coats and although they were noisy enough they were not fanatical. That was one place where we were not accommodated in a five-star hotel; it was more like a well-worn B&B.

Vojvodina surprised us: they were a lot better than we had thought they could be, and turned out to be the best team we played in the European Cup that season. Jock did brief us well before the game. He said that Vojvodina had some good players, were well-disciplined, played well for each other and would be a very hard side to break down. All of that was true and, although I cannot remember them having lot of strikes at goal in the first leg, they did have a lot of the ball and had us chasing about a wee bit. We found it hard to get the ball back off them and once we did, it wasn't too easy to hold on to it. They had good players but no outstanding ones; instead, they played very, very well as a team. I made a bad mistake for their goal over in Novi Sad, when I was short with a pass back to Ronnie Simpson. Their guy intercepted it and knocked it away and we did well to keep the score to 1–0 at the end of the 90 minutes. If you make a mistake like that, the only thing to do is get over it as quickly as possible and do your best to make sure it does not happen again. I was not one for having a hang-up about such things: once it's done it's done and there is nothing you can do about it.

In the second match with Vojvodina, in Glasgow, we had to work really, really hard to get a result. We had to wait until well into the second half before Stevie opened the scoring and, just as we thought we were going to end the game level on aggregate, Billy scored with a header in the final minute. You could probably hear a sigh of relief across Glasgow when we got that winning goal because we certainly didn't look forward to going to a third game, which would have been at a neutral venue; that was how UEFA decided drawn ties in the European Cup at that point. That life-or-death struggle with Vojvodina meant that we regarded reaching the semi-finals as a momentous achievement in itself.

If we could have taken our pick of the other three semi-finalists, we would probably have taken CSKA Sofia, the Bulgarian club, but we were drawn against Dukla Prague, the Czechoslovakian army side. That still suited us fairly well because we had avoided Inter Milan and the Dukla players were possibly slightly past their best. They had a magnificent midfield player, Josef Masopust, but he had turned 36 a couple of months earlier. We won 3–1 in the first leg, at Celtic Park, so we were confident of doing well in the second, but Jock Stein surprised us all in the team talk a couple of days beforehand in Dukla's Juliska Stadium. He gave us the breakdown of how he thought they would play and then came right out and said that we were going to play defensively, with one man up the park, a packed midfield and everyone other than the striker, Stevie Chalmers, funnelling back into defensive positions whenever Dukla had the ball. As he came out with these instructions, all of us began looking at each other in complete bewilderment. We had never heard words like that coming out of Big Jock's mouth – normally his pre-match instructions would be to go into attacking mode at every chance.

There was a strange backdrop to the match in Prague. Every spectator, it seemed, was a soldier. They all had on brown greatcoats, peaked caps and military uniforms. The Czech authorities had obviously told their soldiers to have a day off and go to the game. You would think that if they had been given some time off and had turned out to back up their team, they would be screaming their support but they didn't make a lot of noise and that suited us perfectly. As with Vojvodina, the stadium was fairly modest, but we were well aware that this was only a platform for us to reach the final in Lisbon, which we knew would be a different, much more colourful prospect on the day of the European Cup final.

Jock's tactics worked. Dukla had most of the ball but we choked them and stopped them from really playing. We also clamped down hard on Masopust but, although he was man-marked, he was still knocking balls around with real flair; he was a great passer of the ball, a builder of the game, a bit like Jim Baxter, except with more of a work-rate, and we struggled to control him. We did well enough, though, to prevent them getting in a lot of shots at goal and most of those that they did manage were from about 25 or 30 yards. They never got many real chances inside the box. It was the only time we played defensively in Europe and we should have been given a going-over, so when the final whistle went with the score 0–0 there was real jubilation. We had achieved our ambition to become the first British club to reach the European Cup final. We could relax and enjoy ourselves so we all got bevvied on the flight back.

I think it was an advantage that we avoided meeting the really big names in European football on our run to the final. It gave us a chance to settle into the rhythm of playing European Cup ties and through beating lesser-known teams in the early rounds we began to develop a bit of confidence. Meeting Zurich and Nantes, especially, helped us find our feet in Europe although we got a rude awakening from the tie with Vojvodina. That was the only time in our entire run to the final during that 1966–67 season that I thought that we could be on the verge of elimination from the European Cup.

We knew we had every chance of beating Inter Milan in the final provided we didn't do anything stupid. On arrival in Portugal we checked in at the Hotel Palacio in Estoril, which is about fifteen to twenty minutes outside Lisbon. It had a lovely big swimming pool but as usual Jock wouldn't let us into it. Nor would he let us sit in the sun because he said that would weaken our legs; he really came out with some howlers. So, not being allowed to swim or sunbathe, we would sit in the shade playing cards, which becomes pretty boring after a while. We could see all these people, including the businessmen who habitually travelled along with Celtic, stretched out sunbathing by the pool with parasols up, bottles of wine open, taking the occasional cooling dip and otherwise gently smouldering away. Jock's demand that we sit quietly in the shade was a bit too serious for me and one or two others. So on the afternoon of the Tuesday, the day on which we arrived, Bertie Auld, Willie Wallace and myself jumped in a taxi, went to a village down the road from Estoril called Cascais, found a place called the John Bull, an English pub, and had three pints each before taking a taxi back to Estoril. Jock knew nothing about it.

We were not allowed into the city of Lisbon itself but the businessmen who were with our party did go into town and on their return would tell us that the place was mobbed with Celtic supporters. It gave us a boost to know that we were going to get good backing. I felt fine in the approach to the game; no nerves at all. Once we got to the National Stadium itself, though, we had to wait for several minutes in the tunnel before kick-off, alongside the Italians, and that was the only time when the tension began to build. They were all tanned, with their hair slicked back. Helenio Herrera, their manager, had certainly never told them to stay out of the sun. Wee Jinky said, 'Look at them: they're like film stars.' I said, 'Yes, but can they play?' We were looking them up and down, giving them the Glasgow stare, and it's a bit awkward standing there for five minutes when you cannot speak to them. At last wee Bertie burst into the Celtic Song and we all joined in. The Italians were looking at us as if we were crazy, as if to say, 'Who are these bampots we are playing in a European final?' For us, though, it released the tension because we were getting a bit uptight; we just wanted to be out there on the park and to get on with it.

Inter had won the tournament in 1964 and 1965 so they would have expected to go to Lisbon and beat us. I think they were happy to be facing us in the final; the biggest-spending club in Europe would have anticipated few problems in facing a team from the Scottish League. They would have gone into the match thinking that they were going to control it, and I think they were unpleasantly surprised at what they had to face that day. All you had to do was look at Helenio Herrera's face. He was a picture of fury on the touchline and became more and more so as the game progressed towards its conclusion.

We went behind to a Sandro Mazzola penalty after only seven minutes when Jim Craig fouled Renato Cappellini inside the penalty area. Jim Craig said it wasn't a penalty kick. He's a liar: it was a stonewaller. We didn't say that at the time, mind you. That was probably the best thing that could have happened to us – going behind to them early in the match – because they just sat back and gave us the ball and they were asking for trouble because we had too many potential goal scorers. Our self-confidence never wavered for an instant, even after that setback. They looked confident after their goal and, when they were on top and controlling the game, it was very, very difficult to get the ball off them. That only lasted for ten minutes. After that, we took charge. The number of saves Giuliano Sarti, the Inter goalkeeper, had was nobody's business. In the first half we could quite easily, by rights and without exaggerating, have been 3–1 up but Sarti made some fabulous saves and they carried out some great defending as well, blocking shots and shutting people down in the area 20 yards from goal.

I have never seen a European Cup final in which a team has dominated the match more than in that final in Lisbon. We had so many shots on goal and the only reason Inter were able to keep the score down was because Sarti had such an exceptionally good game. I alone could have had a hat-trick. I hit a shot low to Sarti's left-hand post in the first half and I still don't know how he got to it. I also hit the crossbar late on but that was actually just a cross into the middle that went too long and ended up striking the bar. We had so many strikes on goal that were either very well saved or just off target that we began thinking it might just be one of those games in which you have all the play and never score.

We kept pushing for the equaliser and after 63 minutes it arrived. I was pleased to be the man to make history when I lent my weight to the attack, but at that point I shouldn't have been where I was, up close to the penalty area, because if Jim Craig, who passed the ball to me for my strike on goal, was going forward, I was supposed to be keeping the back door shut, along with Billy and John Clark. At that stage of the game, though, Inter were playing with only one man up: Mazzola. The rest of them fell back into midfield to try to fill the middle of the park and at the back they played their usual *catenaccio* system, in which they had a spare man sitting about ten yards behind the back four. So, with Billy, John Clark and Ronnie at the back, there was no point in my hanging back there doing nothing.

The guy that was supposed to be on me as a marker was Angelo Domenghini and he was so lazy. I would think that he would have been delegated by Herrera to go back with me if I went forward, to cut me out, but that was not happening. None of the Italian players came back with me during the match so I was continually unchallenged as I received diagonal passes from midfield from Bertie and Bobby Murdoch. Nobody marked me for the whole game. It was an easy situation but still hard work because I was back and forward all the time and the heat was stifling.

I had been easing forward throughout the match so when I saw that Jim Craig had also been allowed a free run down the right-hand side, I just set off from our half. He had pushed forward on the right when I began to make my run from the edge of our centre circle. When this situation arose there was nobody in front of me at all so I just made a bee-line through their defence, right through the middle of the park. Jim Craig was free on the right-hand side – he had slipped his marker – and I made a clean run because there was nobody picking me up. The Italians believed in defending in depth in and around the edge of their penalty box, so they had filled their box with bodies. At every turn during the match, they had had bodies crammed inside their box, which they thought gave them safety in numbers. Essentially that was true because in the first half we had had a lot of chances but had never really gone close. Their 'keeper made some good saves but our efforts on goal were from a distance. That was why big Jock told us at half-time that when we were going down either wing we should cut the ball back to the edge of the box instead of firing it in towards the penalty-spot area, which is what we had been doing in the first half. The tactic that Jock outlined was likely to bring us joy because we had players following up from midfield, the likes of myself and Jim, and midfield players like Bertie and Bobby Murdoch backing up the forwards on the edge of the box; so if we got the ball wide on either side of the field we had players ready to shoot for goal when the ball was played back to them.

Three times I shouted to Jim to square it to me but he held it . . . and held it . . . and held it. Finally, he drew another Inter defender out towards him and decided to cut the ball back to me. I was slightly right of centre, on the arc, the 'D', as I prepared to receive the ball. Normally, if the play had been in midfield with Bobby or Bertie I'd have been wide on the left going down the touchline, but because the play was on the right-hand side and there was nobody picking me up, I could just charge forward because there was nothing to lose and I had nobody to pick up. It was great. It was only a ten- or twelve-yard pass that Jim made to me; that was how close I was to him when he cut it back to me diagonally. I would have been about 25 yards out when I was screaming to him for the ball so by the time it got to me I was about 22 or 23 yards out. It was a great pass, right along the deck, and the park was like a bowling green, so it was just a case of timing. He cut it back while I was still making my run and I latched on to it at full tilt.

If you look at the goal, there's a defender, Armando Picchi, the Inter sweeper, who comes out to block the ball but about two yards from me he stops and turns his back. If he had taken one more pace he could have changed Celtic's history. All he had to do was take one more pace and he would have blocked that shot but, as Italians often do, he came out so far and then turned his back, which gave me a free shot at goal. The ball was on the deck and I hit it with my instep. I wasn't aiming for the top right-hand corner. I just wanted to hit the target and hit it as hard as I could, and when I did I was confident that it was on target. The closer you are to goal the less chance there is of it going over the bar. I got right over the top of it and although it was wide of the keeper I don't think it was above shoulder-height. It is possible that Sarti was blinded a wee bit when Picchi came out to shut me out but that wouldn't have mattered if Picchi had advanced further to block the ball. My momentum took me past Picchi and by that time the ball was in the net. At the time, I didn't actually see Picchi coming out – I only noticed him after I had hit the ball – and I never really realised what had happened until I saw it on film when the BBC replayed it a couple of days later. My goal may have looked spectacular but I have never seen a bad goal in my life. Even if it's from two yards out, it's a good goal if it is for your side. Some look better than others and some are more important than others but they are all good. That was the best I ever scored: not only did it look picturesque but it turned the most important match in Celtic's history in our favour.

I was doing handstands. It was a tremendous feeling to score because as soon as the ball hit the net I knew we were going to beat them. When I went back for the restart and into the left-back position it made me the closest man to the dugout and big Jock said, 'Take it easy, we'll take them in extra time.' I said, 'Fuck that, boss. It's eighty-five degrees out here and the sweat is pouring off us. I'm not playing for another half an hour. We're going to beat them now.'

I had my socks at my ankles because of the heat and there was about half an hour to go. It was roasting. You couldn't get a breath; there wasn't even a breeze. And I had been on the go all afternoon because I didn't have anybody marking me. I don't know whether they were trying to get me to push forward and leave spaces into which one of them might be able to creep; if that was their plan they never carried it out. They would not commit enough players forward to do that. Cappellini and Mazzola were the only two, really, that did anything. Inter were so dedicated to their defensive style of play that they couldn't change it and once they were up against it, they couldn't do anything to get themselves back into the game.

They certainly missed Luis Suarez, the Spanish international, who had made news by becoming the most expensive player in world football when Herrera purchased him for Inter from Barcelona in 1961 for £214,000. He was ruled out of the match with us through injury. Suarez was their playmaker – though he wasn't any better a playmaker than Bertie Auld or Bobby Murdoch – and he would have improved Inter's performance by making them tick in midfield and building the game for them, and on the day they didn't have anyone like that in their team, so they couldn't hold on to the ball long enough. With us going forward from all parts of the park, we had them back-pedalling all the time. If Suarez had been fit, Inter might have put us under more pressure, but I am certain that we would still have won the game.

They did have other stars in their Lisbon line-up but the quality of our football was such that they were close to anonymous. Giacinto Facchetti, their left-back, had been the original overlapping full-back but he did nothing on the day of the final. Mazzola, their top goal scorer, was pretty quiet apart from an early flourish. Their attitude to the game was shown from kick-off in the first half: as soon as the game began, a guy called Tarcisio Burgnich, who played at right-back, immediately veered all the way across the park to mark wee Jinky. So Big Jock said to wee Jinky, 'Take him for a walk.' Wee Jimmy took him away, twisting and turning all over the place, to create space, and that is how Jim Craig started to find space down the right-hand side. It also left a gap on the left into which Bobby Murdoch could power forward. Inter were undermined by their own safety-first tactics.

The first thing I said to myself when I saw the ball hit their net from my strike was 'That's it. We've got them now.' In the first half we had given them such a going-over. After they got their penalty kick so early in the game, they had just fallen back and soaked up pressure because they were good at that; they were skilled at defending in depth on the edge of their own box. I think they were only in our half two or three times in the second half. As soon as they scored, they started giving us the ball but we had nine potential goal scorers. Apart from John Clark and Ronnie Simpson, everybody might have scored from free kicks, corner kicks or cut-backs from front players or midfield players. No team in the world could have given us as much of the ball and not lost a goal.

Once we got that goal of mine you could see the look of bewilderment on the Inter players' faces, their hands on their hips and their heads drooping down. So we looked at them and told each other that we really had to go for it. There was a clear difference between their attitude to losing a goal and the attitude we had shown when Mazzola's penalty went in. As soon as we lost that penalty kick, early in the game, the first thing we had said to each other had been, 'Let's get in about these guys!' There was none of that from the Italians after the equaliser. It was strange: you would expect to see a bit of spirit from a team fighting for its life in a European Cup final. We Celts had been at each other's throats every minute of the game, cajoling and shouting and arguing.

Although the score was level at 1–1 and it had taken until midway through the second half for us to score, we had pulverised them. Prior to my goal, they had sat back, content in the knowledge that as long as we didn't score, they were going to win the European Cup, but I think they knew that if we got a goal we were going to get another one. You could see defeat in their faces after it became 1–1. They must also have thought that luck was with them that day. We felt we had had a stonewall penalty kick that hadn't been given when Willie Wallace's leg was grabbed. It was unbelievable: the Inter player had two hands round his leg. At another point, we thought the ball had been behind the line when the keeper had grabbed it.

For our second goal, five minutes from time, I cut the ball back to Bobby Murdoch on the edge of the penalty area and he hit it low in to Stevie, who was where he would normally be in a training session. Stevie simply extended a leg to divert the ball into the net. If it hadn't been Stevie, it would have been wee Bobby Lennox. We practised that in training every day at Barrowfield, and at times Barrowfield could be a bit churned-up, so there was no way we were going to mess up on the lush, smooth turf of the National Stadium. Some people think that second goal was a bit of a fluke, because it looks as if Bobby Murdoch hits a hopeful ball into the six-yard box, but he knew that Stevie would be there to tap it into the net. Four times a week, in training, we had players going down either side and cutting balls back to the likes of myself or Jim Craig or Bobby Murdoch or Bertie Auld or Charlie Gallagher, and Jock would have the front players in on top of the goalkeeper so that if anything was going wide of the goal or across goal, they would just toe-poke it into the net. We scored lots of goals like that every season, through the likes of Stevie or Bobby Lennox. If any loose ball fell in or around the six-yard box, Bobby would be on to it like nobody's business. So that second goal was part of a well-rehearsed routine. The Italians had not wanted to know after it had become 1–1 and when our second one went in they were looking for the referee to blow the whistle. We had had them under pressure for more or less the entire game. They were chasing shadows.

I think we had expected more of a game from Inter, more resistance. We couldn't believe that this was the Inter Milan that had won the European Cup a couple of times. We had expected them to take possession more, and were shocked that we were able to dominate the game as much as we did. It was still physically demanding because of the running we had had to do to establish our domination, and the heat. It helped that we were a young team, except for Ronnie Simpson, who was 36. I was 23. Bobby Murdoch, myself and Jimmy Johnstone were all born within six months of each other. Bobby Lennox is only six months older than us. Jim Craig is also the same age as me. John Clark and Willie Wallace were 26, Billy McNeill was 27 and Bertie Auld 29. Stevie Chalmers was the oldest member of the team after Ronnie but he was still only 30.

It was 45 minutes before I could get off the pitch after the match. Ten thousand Celtic supporters were in the crowd and it seemed as if most of them were on the field of play at the end. As the match had been drawing closer to the final whistle, we had been awarded a free kick and wee Bertie had said to me, 'What are you going to do with it?' I said, 'Do you see that fucking moat, twenty yards behind the goal? It is going straight in there.' That is exactly what I did and a few seconds later, after Sarti had taken the goal kick, the referee blew his whistle for the conclusion of the game. It meant that I was up on the edge of the Inter box, having just taken that free kick, so I was at the opposite end of the field from the dressing room and I had no chance of getting off the pitch swiftly once it became swamped by Celtic supporters. I still don't know how they managed to negotiate the moat that was supposed to prevent people leaving the terraces and getting on to the field of play. I had exchanged jerseys with Sandro Mazzola after the whistle and there were a number of supporters seeking my jersey, boots and so on but I was not for letting go of them. A guy with whom I was friendly, John O'Donnell, who owned Mount Vernon dog track, along with one of his pals, got his arms around me and helped stop the other fans getting at my gear. The Portuguese cops were great because they let the fans mill around on the pitch and didn't overreact, which was the right thing to do because the fans were not causing any harm.

Eventually, just I was about to enter the tunnel, I spied Billy away up at the top of the main stand, receiving the trophy. In the dressing room there were two or three female photographers – the first time I had ever seen that in a football dressing room – and the guys were all walking around naked saying, 'Go on, my darling', and all that sort of stuff. Most of the guys had lost their jerseys, boots, pants and socks to the supporters but I had managed to keep mine.

Then the partying began. There was an official UEFA dinner at a beautiful restaurant in Lisbon. Inter were more than two hours late – Herrera must have been laying into them – and the UEFA officials were fuming. By the time Inter arrived we were all pissed and gave them a sardonic round of applause. Our wives and girlfriends had gone to another restaurant so, after the UEFA banquet, we joined them and had a few drinks with them. We then accompanied the girls to Lisbon Airport because they were scheduled to fly home that evening.

I had arranged with John O'Donnell, when he rescued me on the park, that I would meet up with him later that evening at the Texas Bar. There was a square mile of Lisbon where all the bars were named after American states. So as the Celtic coach made its way from the airport across Lisbon and back to Estoril, I said to big Jock, 'Boss, stop the bus.' He said, 'Where do you think you're going?' I said, 'Boss, I've arranged to meet three good friends of mine in the centre of Lisbon. Can you stop the bus?' So, reluctantly, he allowed me to disembark and the rest of the players went back to Estoril to the hotel. John O'Donnell and his pals had a table booked in prime position inside the club and there was a cabaret going on. The place was full of Celtic supporters, the drink was flowing freely and there were hookers everywhere. I didn't get a minute's peace from the Celtic supporters or the hookers. I was happy to celebrate with the supporters and the hookers were an entertaining enough eyeful but I was never tempted to do any more than enjoy looking at them because I was too pissed. It was a great way to round off the day.

At six in the morning I took a taxi back to the Hotel Palacio and, just as I was arriving, saw a string of taxis leaving the hotel. My fiancée, Anne Deas, who was to become my wife later that year, had been given a green-and-white-hooped dress and coat by the *Daily Express* to model for the newspaper and to wear at the game. So when I saw this green-and-white coat going past me in the opposite direction in another taxi, I said to myself, 'What's happening here?' I found out that after we had left the girls at the airport, a fault had been discovered in one of their aeroplane's engines, delaying their flight by several hours, and big Jock, hearing of this, had ordered a string of taxis to take the girlfriends and wives back to the hotel.

So Anne, on arriving at the hotel, had said, 'Where's Tommy?' Jock had said, 'He's knackered; he's away to his bed. You come to my room with Jean and Rae and have a drink with us.' Then, at six in the morning, when their flight was ready to depart, Anne saw me arriving back at the hotel when I was supposed to be in my bed exhausted. When I got back to Glasgow, she asked me for an explanation and I told her that I had been doing a story for the *Daily Express*. There was a grain of truth in that: I had done a story for the *Express* but I had spoken to their journalist on the plane home rather than in Lisbon. The story did appear, two days after the final, and that seemed to be adequate proof for Anne of what I had said.

We had received a tremendous send-off from Lisbon Airport: we were sped through with the European Cup and treated like the celebrities we had become. At home, the club's officials had asked supporters not to go to the airport in Glasgow to meet us. Instead, they put in the papers the route that our coach would follow in taking us back to Celtic Park from the airport. This was long before the M8 motorway was built so Paisley Road West was the main route into Glasgow from the airport and we had to drive past

Ibrox Park. So we stopped the bus for a few seconds outside Ibrox just to perform a little salute. The whole route was lined with people, and when we got to Celtic Park there appeared to be around 25,000 outside the ground, whilst inside, the stadium was packed to capacity to watch us parade the trophy around the track on an open-topped truck. Back home in Craigneuk, the bunting had been hung from the windows of my parents' house on to the lampposts and the house was jam-packed. I had to send out for a new carry-out on four occasions. The local parish priest, who didn't drink, sank a bottle of sherry, ended up pissed and had to leave his car behind. The man who had been instrumental in starting up Meadow Thistle, Terry Scott, was there with another three of the committee, so it was nice for them because they had started me off in the game.

We didn't get a lot of rest after the final. The match was on Thursday, we got home on Friday, were given Saturday and Sunday off and were back in training on Monday because we were going to play Real Madrid in Alfredo Di Stefano's testimonial a couple of weeks later. So we had to stay in shape for that because we didn't want to go there and fail to do ourselves justice after having become champions of Europe. We did ourselves proud, beating them 1–0 in their own midden in front of 135,000. Three seasons before, we would never have dreamed that anything like that 1966–67 season was possible. Not only had we won the European Cup, the prize of prizes, but we had won every one of the domestic trophies in Scotland. We had lost just three times: to Vojvodina in the European Cup, and twice in the League, both times, strangely enough, to Dundee United. I had played in every one of the 59 matches in all four major competitions that season and had scored sixteen goals. Life was sweet.

Winning the European Cup gave us all more confidence in our ability and produced the odd perk. At the time my mother was working for Billy Skelly, who was from a family who were big car dealers in Motherwell. Billy had been one of the businessmen staying at the Hotel Palacio in Lisbon and had said to me before the final, 'If you score, you are on fifty free gallons of petrol.' I had forgotten all about it when, a week later, I went into his garage where my mother was working on the petrol pumps . She said,

'Mr Skelly says you have to get fifty gallons of petrol.' So I said, 'I'll have six right now.'

Decades after the final, Giuliano Sarti was over for one of the Lisbon Lion reunions and, at the 2002 European Cup final between Bayer Leverkusen and Real Madrid, in Glasgow, we met Giacinto Facchetti and one or two others from that Inter team. They all said that we had been too good for them in 1967. Sarti, in fact, when we met him, held up his hand and stuck up five fingers to show that it should have been five. It was politic of him to do that at our reunion but politic or not, he was right.

5. LIFE AS A LION

home that night and things moved on even more quickly from that point. She soon became my first steady girlfriend.

Anne worked as a hairdresser in Renfield Street and her family were reasonably well-off. Her father, Hamish, was a Highlander, from Sutherland, and her mother, Margaret, a nursing matron, was from Inverness. They were a lovely couple, always very kind to me, and were delighted that Anne and I had got together. I never felt that there was any resentment at me being from a lower-class background, or that they thought I was not good enough to marry their daughter. Hamish was a controller on the railways, quite an important, high-profile job, and had a few bob in stocks and shares that he had inherited from his old man, so Anne, who was an only child, didn't want for anything. Her family may have been middle class but they weren't snobs: her father would go for a drink with the boys after finishing work at West Regent Street and come home at nine o'clock three sheets to the wind. He would fall asleep and Anne and Margaret would then go through his pockets and siphon off a few notes from the wad of money he always carried with him. He would wake up the next morning, count his money and believe he had spent too much again at the pub. He would never know anything about it. Neither Hamish nor Margaret was football-minded and they never came to any of the matches.

I had not known anything about Anne's background when I met her but I believe it was probably only my position as a Celtic footballer that attracted her to me. It wasn't as if I was a film star but in my early twenties I was pretty bubbly and had a bit of personality, and everyone was talking about flamboyant Tommy Gemmell, so I tried to live up to that when I was having a night out. I proposed to her pretty quickly, on the evening of 24 April 1965, just a few hours after we had beaten Dunfermline Athletic in the Scottish Cup final. In those days guys and girls were getting married at eighteen, nineteen or twenty, so we were atypical in having waited until we were 23. A lot of marriages in the '60s may have been spoiled by being made too early: young people had barely begun living before, all of a sudden, they had the handcuffs on them. Then, when they matured, they wanted to take them off.

I still kept in touch with my friends from school and Ravenscraig and I had two stag parties, one for the players and one for my pals, in different hotels. I didn't want the players to go out for my stag night and be pestered by being asked to talk football all night, which, quite understandably, is what my pals would have wanted to do, as they were all football supporters.

We were married in June 1967 at Stamperland Parish Church in Clarkston. I could not believe the scenes at the wedding: there were hundreds of Celtic supporters outside a Proddy church. It was quite moving. The fans were wonderful and gave us a tremendous reception, yelling and shouting; this was, after all, only a few weeks after the European Cup final. The minister who married us told us it was the biggest crowd he had ever had in his church. We had the reception at the Vesuvio, an Italian restaurant in St Vincent Place where the Celtic players always used to go after matches. The three Italian partners who ran the restaurant were brilliant guys, real football fanatics: Mario, Umberto and Enzo. They put on a fantastic reception for us. The bottom tier of the wedding cake was an iced replica of the National Stadium in Lisbon, with players in the green and white hoops of Celtic and others in the black and blue stripes of Inter. That was the partners' idea and it was a wonderful touch. Although they were Italian they were quite happy that we had beaten Inter because they were from Naples.

Mario, Umberto and Enzo ran two top-notch restaurants, the Vesuvio and the Sorrento in Buchanan Street, which is now the Caprese. The food in both was prepared to perfection. If we were going out into town for an evening meal, those two and the Rogano were our favourite dining places. We would never be pestered or have any hassle in there. All of the first-team players received an invitation to my wedding but four or five of them couldn't make it because they were already booked on holidays; at that time you booked your holidays about nine months in advance. Quite a lot of the guys did come along, as did Jock Stein, Neilly Mochan and Bob Rooney. Everyone enjoyed it.

Lloret de Mar was the venue for our honeymoon and who was in the same hotel but Willie Waddell, who had been a player for Rangers and, as manager of Kilmarnock, had won the Scottish League title in 1965. By 1967 he had become a sportswriter for the *Daily Express*. I had a few chinwags with him about the

European Cup final, big Jock and football in general. He seemed OK to me but when I got back home I found out that he had written a story in the *Express* in which I was quoted as being critical of big Jock. I had been under the impression that I had been talking off the record and in complete confidentiality to Waddell; after all, he and his wife were also on holiday. Essentially, Waddell broke a confidence between us but once a story is there in print there is little you can do about it. Waddell later stabbed in the back Davie White, the Rangers manager in the late '60s, by slaughtering him on numerous occasions in the paper and suggesting that he wasn't up to the job. White was soon sacked and Waddell replaced him as manager shortly afterwards. That, I would say, tells you something about the man. Willie Henderson told me that shortly after Waddell became Rangers manager, Willie was asked by an intermediary if he would like to play in South Africa during the summer. Willie replied to the South Africans' representative that Waddell would never allow it but was told that Waddell had already agreed that it would not be a problem. Willie went to see Waddell to ask what was going on and Waddell said to him, 'You can play wherever you like. I am giving you a free transfer.' That was a strange way to treat a player who had served Rangers with distinction for twelve years.

With marriage, a host of responsibilities dropped on my doorstep. I bought a house on Market Road in Kirkintilloch, so I had a mortgage to pay and a wife to look after; then our daughter, Karen Michelle, was born in November 1967. I had still been doing a bit of philandering in the West End whilst engaged to Anne but once I was married the wild nights were all over. Marriage put the brakes on carefree, harebrained behaviour; for a while anyway. I didn't get involved in changing nappies but I quite happily went out wheeling the pram. Anne gave up work after she had the baby and became a housewife because I was earning a good bit more than a tradesman and could pay the mortgage. We could buy whatever clothes we wished and dine out and have a drink when we wanted without incurring any financial hardship. We could even be a wee bit extravagant and go out two or three times a week. I always had enough money in the bank to keep me going in style and at Celtic we knew we were almost guaranteed to receive win bonuses every week.

Our basic wage in 1967, when we won the European Cup, was £40 per week. The bonus for a League win was £10, with £5 for a draw. Things were different with cup-tie bonuses: if we won a cup tie, we never knew what our bonus was going to be for winning that game until the draw was made for the following round. Then big Desmond White, the club secretary, would work out how much we were likely to earn from gate money for the succeeding tie and, on that basis, work out the bonus for the game that we had already won. If we won the Scottish Cup we would get about £250. That sum looks good but it would be taxed. We paid the normal rate of tax, 33 per cent, but, depending on what you had earned up to that point in the year, the taxman would also deduct surtax – so the government took a big chunk of any sizeable win bonus. We received a bonus of £1,500 for winning the European Cup and once tax and surtax had been deducted, I finished up with £720. There was nothing you could do about that other than emigrate. I spent £120 of what was left on a Rolex watch from Laing's, the jewellers, in Renfield Street, a watch that I still wear today. I gave £100 to Anne and I bought a new Ford Cortina for £500 from Skellys in Motherwell, where my mother worked. That was it; gone, wiped out. At the peak of your career as a footballer, when you're flying high, winning more or less every game and making good money, you think that it will never end.

Kirkintilloch was a great place in which to live. We had a three-bedroomed detached villa on the edge of the town, only a fifteen-minute drive from Celtic Park, close to the countryside but still not far from the city. We had great neighbours. The only real problem was the milk boy, who chanted 'Gemmell's a bastard' at seven o'clock every morning as he carried out his delivery. I did not tolerate that for very long before I got him sacked; that was not my idea of an early-morning alarm call. One minor drawback was that Kirkintilloch did not have any pubs. I didn't know that before I bought the house; if I had, I might have chosen somewhere else to live.

Cars were my biggest indulgence during my time as a footballer. From the time I joined Celtic until the time I stopped playing football, I owned twenty different cars, although never more than one at a time. Cars were a necessity, both as a means of getting around and as part of your image. The one I enjoyed best was a magnificent, white, S-type Jaguar which I bought in 1968; it was almost identical to the present-day S-type. I went on an ego trip when I got that; my head had swollen with our success at Celtic and I felt that the S-type would fit right in with my image as a flair player. I knew it would impress all the guys at the Park and the supporters – and it did. It was great fun to drive up there in that gleaming S-type with the punters all giving you the thumbs up as you motored past them. Better than riding up to the ground on a bicycle, isn't it? I think that the punters enjoyed seeing me arriving in style even though a lot of them would not have had cars themselves. Occasionally, I found my beautiful car had been scraped by nails or keys but you've got to expect that.

Wearing the right gear was just as important. I fell victim to all the fashions of those flower-power days: bell-bottoms, flares, striped shoes, shirt collars that came halfway down your chest and clothes in every garish colour you can imagine. I cringe, now, looking back at it, but that type of gear was top dog at that time and if you wore all the latest fashions you were king of the road. The most outrageous outfit I wore was striped, flared trousers and black-and-white-striped shoes. There was a shirtmaker in Glasgow, with premises at the top of Buchanan Street, who provided made-to-measure shirts for all the Celtic players. His was the in place to go for beautifully made shirts and everybody in Glasgow who was recognisable in the late 60s went to him. They were all in the flower-power style with paisley patterns, loud enough to shout at passers-by. The shirts he made for the Celtic players had our initials on the pocket and when we went on holiday, to places such as Minorca, Majorca and Lloret de Mar, all the punters wanted to buy the shirts simply because they had our initials on them. I used to get myself a right few quid in pesetas, probably double what I had originally paid for the shirt. Would I have been involved in that scene if I had still been an electrician at Ravenscraig? No, so I made sure I made the best of it. We worked hard and played hard at the right times. It was always a hard shift in training at Celtic Park so you earned your fun and that made me all the more determined to enjoy my time off as much as possible.

The hippy thing was at its peak during that era but never at any time in my life have I been involved in drugs. I've never smoked, for starters, so there was little chance that I would try marijuana, let alone cocaine or heroin. At the very start of my career at Celtic Park, a couple of first-team players dabbled in amphetamines; if they were having a social drink they would have a couple of these pills and it would put them on a high. But I never indulged in that sort of thing and, as far as I am aware, neither did any of my team-mates in the Lisbon Lions. We just stuck to the booze. We did like the music, such as The Beatles and The Rolling Stones, and Nat King Cole, Dean Martin and Frank Sinatra were still going strong. There were some great female singers at that time too, such as Nancy Wilson. I never saw any of those big '60s acts live but there was a good mixture of music in the air, made up of both the new rock music and the more melodic acts, and it provided a great soundtrack to our lives, which we were living to the limit.

We lived it up, but we also knew how far we could go with Stein and with the public. We had a smashing lifestyle that the guy in the street could not afford but it was important not to rub people's noses in that or to become in any way superior. Jock was clever inasmuch as he never attempted to change our lifestyles; if we were still playing high-quality football, there was no reason for him to interfere with our lives off the pitch.

You had to be careful where you spent your leisure time when you were a Celtic player. You could not go anywhere you wished. After matches, on a Saturday night, three or four of us would go for a drink and we had to choose the venue carefully. We used to go to the Rogano because it was a wee bit upmarket and there would be no troublemakers in there. At other pubs, popular pubs in Gordon Street or West Nile Street, you would be sitting having a drink and people would come up and start saying stupid things like 'What about that tackle you made on so-and-so today . . . that was a disgrace.' You'd say, 'Do you mind, boys? The game's over. We just want a nice, wee, quiet drink to relax and unwind.' They would keep on so we would just look at each other, put our drinks down and walk out.

Sean Connery, who was at the height of his stardom as James Bond in the '60s, attended a lot of our matches. He was friendly with big Jock and would come down to see us at the Marine Hotel or Seamill when we were preparing for a match or having a break. He would have a game of golf and say hello to the boys. He would also be brought into the dressing room by Big Jock before matches to shake hands and wish us all the best. That gave everyone a lift. We were stars in our own right but we were plankton compared to one of the biggest fish in the movie world of the '60s. He was very friendly and also very modest; you would never have known he was one of the hottest young properties in the movie business. In fact, he was quite introverted. The boys appreciated him being so down to earth. He came across as being very much a Celtic supporter, but now he appears to have jumped the dyke and is pally with David Murray, the Rangers chairman.

We also met Richard Attenborough when we played in Los Angeles against Atlas of Mexico on our tour of North America in 1966. It was roasting hot that day, in the high nineties, and Richard Attenborough came into our dressing room before the match, looking very dapper in suit, shirt and tie, walked down the tunnel with us as we went out for the game, watched it and came back into the dressing room to congratulate us afterwards. I don't know how big Jock managed to dig up these celebrities and persuade them to associate with us but it did add a touch of style to proceedings.

Among the other characters associated with Celtic in the 60s was the bookmaker Tony Queen, who was a close friend and confidant of big Jock. Tony knew what we were all getting up to away from the Park but he always kept quiet about it. He loved Jock's company but he loved the patter of the players even more; he preferred being in among all the guys in the team because we would wind him up and wind up each other. The quips would be crackling through the air as fast as electricity. He and two or three of his cronies would always fly to European away matches with the team and we would just carry out wind-ups on them. They loved it. It got to the stage where they weren't supporters but friends. Jock would tell Tony things that Tony was supposed to keep to himself but Tony would come up to us individually and say, 'I'm not supposed to tell you this but . . .' One day he came up to me and said, 'I'm going to tell you something that big Jock said to me the other day but don't you ever repeat it. He told me that you are the best left-back in the world.' I said, 'Oh, that's good to know, Tony.' I don't believe that Jock knew Tony was telling us all these stories because once you lost Jock's confidence he wouldn't tell you anything else.

Dick Beattie, a goalkeeper who had been with Celtic when I had joined as a youngster, was later jailed for match-fixing after he had moved to English football, but nobody ever approached me to throw games or anything like that. As a footballer, you did run into one or two people who had clubs in Glasgow and, you might say, could be regarded as shady characters. There was a guy called Hughie O'Donnell who had the Raven Club in Renfrew Street. To describe it as seedy would be an understatement. Hughie's face was criss-crossed with scars but a nicer guy you couldn't meet. He would always invite me to go to the Raven so I went up two or three times. It was an illegal gambling den, with unlicensed booze and hookers everywhere, but it was jam-packed. There were two heavies on the door, which was little more than a slit in the wall. 'You've got to be a member to get in here, son,' they growled at me the first time I approached the club. Inside, it was completely black; there was no lighting. If you walked in there on your own at night, you would be looking over your shoulder, but after my first visit Hughie would arrange for a couple of heavies to meet me somewhere and take me up to the club with them.

I shudder to think what the club would have been like normally, because when I went there Hughie made sure I saw it at its best. 'We're just having a wee drink and a wee game of poker,' he would say, but the club was a front for a whole lot of things that I didn't find out about until later. I'm talking about organised crime and drugs. The cops knew that the club was there and what was going on but they weren't too unhappy about it because at least they knew that all these characters were in one place and controlled to some extent. They would occasionally raid it to keep up appearances, but Hughie had an alarm bell on the door; on sight of the cops, the panic button would be pressed, the cards would go under the table and the booze would go out the window. Hughie came to all the Celtic games and was a smashing guy but he got on the wrong side of a few people somewhere along the line. He went to London and someone handed him out some severe punishment: they knocked his eye out. I later bumped into him at Piccadilly Circus and he was his normal self, as if nothing had happened.

That was the nearest I got to the crime scene; I was more often to be found in an altogether more healthy environment as I went in pursuit of the hunting, shooting and fishing lifestyle. That had first caught my interest when I had been serving my apprenticeship at Ravenscraig. George Devine, the brother of the Scottish country-and-western singer Sydney Devine, worked alongside me and he was friendly with a gamekeeper on an estate in Clelland, which is only four miles from Craigneuk. George asked me if I would like to come along with him one night to shoot some pigeons. That was the first time I had ever been involved in anything to do with shooting. There were four guys shooting these wood pigeons out of the air and I thought it was unbelievable how they could shoot them down so accurately; I didn't know that there were 100 pellets coming out of the gun and fanning out into the air every time it was fired. So the following week I went out with them again and this time I shot some pigeons and wild duck and that was me hooked.

I later did a favour for a friend of mine when I got a black Labrador pup for his brother, who worked on an estate in Perthshire. The brother appreciated what I had done for him and introduced me to some farmer pals of his, one of whom owned a pub to the north of Perth. Talk got round to shooting and fishing and they told me to give them a shout whenever I wanted to indulge in some countryside sport. So I got started on some serious hunting. I would go to four different farms in the Perthshire area to shoot pheasant, duck, geese, rabbit, hare, pigeon and grouse. I used to beg a day off from big Jock to go shooting and invariably he would say it would be fine. I would then take him in a couple of pheasants the following morning. Wee Jinky and Bertie Auld got the urge to become involved in the hunting and shooting so on the odd occasion I would take them along with me and they loved it. I had a pal who owned the

Smiddy Haugh Inn, just near Aberirvine, which is only three or four miles from where we were shooting, and he used to put us up for dinner, bed and breakfast. His wife would make us an enormous steak dinner and Bertie, myself, Jinky and three other pals would go in there after the shooting, give them a couple of pheasants for the pot, enjoy a superb dinner and then have a monumental piss-up. They were good fun days and excellent exercise. Shooting is hard work: you are not just standing on the spot shooting birds; you have to walk through woods and up and down ditches to hunt them down.

It was great to get away out into the country and in amongst wildlife. The only wildlife I had known as a boy in Craigneuk had been sparrows and crows. It was a very pleasant change of scenery. The farmers were smashing guys and every time we played St Johnstone, Dundee or Dundee United I would fix up tickets for them. I later got to know some farmers on the Tay who owned stretches of the river for fishing and I enjoyed salmon and trout fishing free of charge. Some people think fishing is boring but it is the fastest day in the world. You start fishing in the morning and, before you know it, it's four o'clock in the afternoon because you are concentrating so closely on trying to land a fish.

It seemed as if there was little that could go wrong for me as a European Cup winner and a first-choice first-team player for Celtic. Jock Stein rated me highly and with him at the helm there was every reason to believe that Celtic's domination of the Scottish game would continue and that the club would maintain a high-profile presence in European football. We harboured serious ambitions to win a second and even a third European Cup. I was earning well and taking great pleasure in every aspect of my life and I felt that even though I might commit the occasional misdemeanour, I had a healthy relationship with Jock. I thought that he was a mature enough manager to realise that I more than made up for any off-field indiscretions with the effort, commitment and ability that I could offer him on the park. It would not be long before those beliefs were severely undermined.

6. NATIONAL SERVICE

Well, that day, Archie Gourlay helped me unravel a large part of that mystery. No wonder we never qualified for World Cup finals or European Nations Cup finals.

I won my first cap against England at Hampden in April 1966 – it was a magnificent occasion and a great game. We were playing against the nucleus of the English World Cup-winning side: nine of the English team that would win the World Cup three months later faced us on that day in Glasgow. Unfortunately, they beat us 4–3 but they needed Nobby Stiles to head the ball off the line in the final minute to make sure of their win. So we didn't do too badly against a team that was going to be world champions within weeks. Jimmy Johnstone scored twice for us that day and it was fantastic to get my first cap at Hampden in an exceptionally exciting match. There were six Old Firm players in that Scotland team: myself, John Greig, Bobby Murdoch, Ronnie McKinnon, Jimmy and Willie Johnston plus Jim Baxter, an honorary Old Firm man who will forever be associated with Rangers but who by 1967 had moved on to Sunderland. Willie Wallace of Hearts was one of our forwards and by the end of that year he would have become a Celtic player. The other three players were Denis Law of Manchester United, Billy Bremner of Leeds United and Bobby Ferguson, the goalkeeper, of Kilmarnock. It is always a great occasion when you play for Scotland against any opposition but to get my first cap against England at Hampden was tremendous.

The Scottish national team at that time was quite frequently 40 per cent Celtic and 40 per cent Rangers with the remainder made up of 'Anglos' – Scottish players with English clubs. The Celtic and Rangers players got to know each other well because we would all mix happily when we were with the Scottish squad prior to an international. The squad used to meet at the Queen's Hotel in Largs, which would be reserved for us alone. We would train in the morning and be given free time in the afternoon but there would be no messing about: we'd be resting in the hotel, playing cards or watching the horse racing on the telly. Big Ronnie McKinnon, the Rangers centre-half, used to do his stint as a bookie and we stitched him up left, right and centre because he didn't understand the basics of bookmaking. We would all pick different horses and put a certain amount on each horse at different prices but he couldn't add up whether he, as bookmaker, was going to come out on top when he looked at the odds and the amount that everyone had bet on each horse. Invariably, he lost with every race. He may have been quick enough on the park but he wasn't the fastest person up top that I've ever met.

Wee Willie Henderson was the worst in terms of goading us to pull another fast one on Ronnie. He constantly encouraged us to rig the betting to ensure that whichever horse won the race Ronnie would still end up as a loser. We did that quite a few times and Ronnie never worked it out. He'd say, 'I'm always losing here . . .' Ronnie and Willie Henderson were always arguing; they didn't like each other, I think because their wives had fallen out. During Celtic v. Rangers matches, I would be marking wee Willie and as soon as Ronnie McKinnon got the ball, Willie would say, 'Wait until you see this, sir . . .' Invariably, Ronnie would try to clear the ball and would end up smacking it into the stand. Wee Willie would say, 'Look at that, sir. What is that all about?' He used to give Ronnie terrible stick.

The camaraderie between Celtic and Rangers players when we were on Scotland trips was exceptional, but it was also good to meet up with Scots who were playing for English clubs – and at that time we had players with all the major clubs in England. It was interesting to find out what life was like for them down south and we discovered that the English-based players were being paid three or four times as much as we were. They would be baffled that we were European Cup winners but were receiving only £45 per week when they were getting £160 or £180. It was a little bit unsettling to hear how much they were earning, especially when none of the major English teams were of the same standard as Celtic at that time. They would tell us to get ourselves down to England to make some real money but that would not have been so easy, even if we had wanted to move, because you only left your club when they wanted you to leave. If your club wanted to hold on to you, they simply did, even when your contract was up, because they retained the option to keep you as their registered player. You were bound to them.

With the English-based players having all that extra cash, it meant that some of the card schools saw some heavy gambling taking place. When it got too heavy, I got out. Card schools with Celtic were a good deal tamer since we limited ourselves to ten shillings (50p) bets.

The Scotland manager when I made my debut was John Prentice and I would have to say he was not outstanding. Malcolm MacDonald, a Celtic player of the '40s, had introduced me to international football with the Scotland Under-23 team, and it was Jock Stein who was manager when I was introduced to the full international squad. During the second half of 1965, Jock had become Scotland's caretaker-manager following the departure of Ian McColl from the manager's post. Scotland were desperately trying to qualify for the 1966 World Cup finals, so Ian McColl had been eased out in the middle of the year and Jock had taken over for the final qualifying matches. Jock had included me in a few Scotland squads, such as the World Cup qualifying match against Italy at Hampden in November 1965, but he had never played me in a match. He told me in advance that although he was putting me in the squad he was not going to play me; it was simply to give me a wee bit of experience. He had, though, been half-thinking of playing me against Italy in the return World Cup qualifier in Naples in December 1965, which Scotland had needed to win to go through, but he told me after the game, which Scotland lost 3–0, that he had decided not to put me in the team because the Italian outside-right was of such a high calibre that I would have been unable to cope with him. That was a reasonable decision on his part and it was fair of Jock to tell me about it.

At that time, the Home International Championship – involving Scotland, Wales, Northern Ireland and England – took place every year and had considerable importance. Matches between Scotland and England would be sold out long in advance and anticipated keenly. The World Cup was important to the British but it only took place every four years, whilst the European Nations Cup – the original name for the European Championships – only involved four teams in the finals and was nothing like as massive as it is today. So the Home Internationals were taken very seriously, particularly our annual match with England, which to us was as important as any World Cup qualifier or European

ove Where it all began:
re I am (*second from the
ft in the front row*) in the
aigneuk Public School
otball team which won
e District Cup in 1953.
uthor's collection)

ght Fit as a fiddle:
orking as well as playing
ver seemed to sap my
ery as you can see. but
e given up jumping over
e garden gate as I used
in 1961!
Empics)

Left The start of something good: celebrating our 3–2 victory over Dunfermline Athletic in the 1965 Scottish Cup final; the win that sparked off the numerous successes of the Jock Stein years at Celtic. *From left:* Ian Young, John Hughes, Stevie Chalmers, John Clark, Billy McNeill (with trophy), Bertie Aulde me, Bobby Lennox, Charlie Gallagher and John Fallon (courtesy of Daily Record)

Below Tuning in: John Hughes, physio Bob Rooney, Jimmy Johnstone and I listen in eagerly to cup draw on the radio at Celtic Park in the mid-1960s.
(Author's collection)

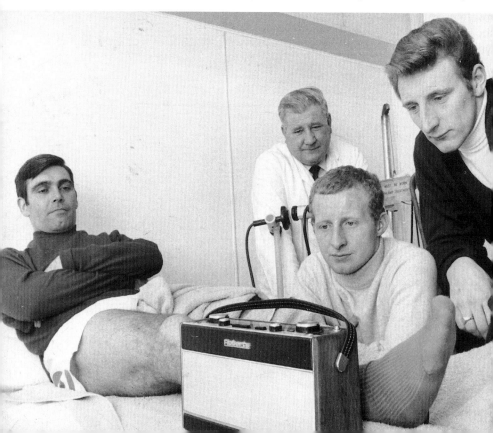

Left A Spanish fiesta: the Celtic team arrives in Madrid, in June 1967, to participate in the testimonial match for the great Argentinian Alfredo Di Stefano. *Clockwise from top left:* Willie O'Neil, Bobby Lennox, Alfredo Di Stefano, Davie Cattanach, Billy McNeill and me. (Author's collection)

Right End of an era: I was always proud to play for my country, but my sending off for Scotland against West Germany in Hamburg in 1969 changed my career. (Courtesy of Daily Record)

Right Getting off to a good start: I open the scoring with a penalty against Racing Club in Buenos Aires in the second leg of the 1967 World Club Championship. The goalkeeper, Cejas, was already several yards off his line as I struck the ball but the power in the shot beat him. (Author's collection)

Above A little bit of history: I was delighted to become one of the few people to have scored twice in a European Cup final. The downside was that we eventually lost to Feyenoord in 1970. (© Empics)

visit to England: a fashionably hirsute Martin O'Neill (*second from left in the middle w*) sits next to me (*third from left*) during my year-and-a-half-long spell at Nottingham rest in the early 1970s. John Robertson, now Martin O'Neill's assistant at Celtic, is rd from the right in the back row. (Courtesy of Daily Record)

Above Ready for action: with the Dundee squad prior to the 1974–75 season, with th[e] League Cup on display. I'm seventh from the right in the front row, flanked by strikers Gordon Wallace, on my right, and John Duncan, on my left. Jocky Scott is to the left of John Duncan and Gordon Strachan (then only seventeen) is far right on the end of the front row. (Courtesy of Daily Record)

Left Management material: keeping a close eye on Jimmy Johnstone, my former Celtic team-mate, as he performs som[e] of his on-field tricks after [I] had made him one of my first signings in my new role as Dundee manager [in] the summer of 1977. (Courtesy of Daily Record[)]

Right Friendly opponent[:] Alan Ball was indeed a fiery opponent of mine fo[r] England and Arsenal during our playing days, but he is now a good friend and, as I have discovered, a great guy. Here we are on a visit to meet fans in Qatar in 2001. (Author's collection)

ove Wedded bliss: Mary and I on our
dding day in 1986
uthor's collection)

Above Teeing off: golf has become one of
my favourite pastimes and here I am
steadying myself for an iron shot whilst
playing in Aberdeen. (Author's collection)

Above Gone fishing: I love fishing too and it was great to see a result on this trip to Dubai. (Author's collection)

Above Keeping it in the family: with my son David, a qualified SFA coach and assistant coach at Stirling Albion at Stirling's Forthbank Stadium in the summer of 2004. (Courtesy of Daily Record)

A proud moment: with other ex-Celts after being voted part of the greatest-ever Celtic team by Celtic supporters. *From left:* Bobby Lennox, Henrik Larsson, Kenny Dalglish, Paul McStay, Jimmy Johnstone, Bertie Auld, Billy McNeill, me, Danny McGrain and Ronnie Simpson. (Author's collection)

Nations Cup match. Over the course of a season, we would play England, Northern Ireland and Wales once, home or away in alternate years, to see who could be British champions. The match with England was one of the few 'live' matches on television in the '60s and the focus of huge attention, so it had been quite special to have been involved in the 1966 fixture.

A Home International with Wales brought me my second Scotland cap and, while I was pleased with that, it is also the saddest memory of my time as a Scotland player. We had travelled down to Cardiff on a Thursday in October 1966 and the Aberfan disaster happened while we were there preparing for the match. On the Friday morning, a waste tip slid down a mountainside into the mining village of Aberfan, near Merthyr Tydfil in South Wales. It destroyed a farm cottage in its path, killing all the occupants, then engulfed a school and a number of houses in the village, killing 144 people. The authorities were talking about cancelling the game and the Welsh Football Association asked the general public, through the media, if they would like the game to be cancelled. The public said not. There was a really eerie atmosphere inside Ninian Park that day, especially when they sang 'Land of My Fathers', their national anthem, before the game. The tears were streaming down everybody's face, including my own: 116 children had perished in that disaster. We drew 1–1 with them that day, Denis Law scored a scrappy goal for us, but it was a very sad occasion and it was difficult to concentrate on the game, especially as the rain, which had caused the whole landslide, was still pouring down. It took some time to get over the experience of that day and it stays with me still.

John Prentice had remained Scotland manager for my first three international matches – against England, Wales and Northern Ireland – but by 1967, when I was awarded my fourth cap, against England at Wembley, Bobby Brown had become the third successive former Rangers player to become full-time Scotland manager, following Ian McColl and John Prentice. Bobby Brown's team talk would consist of a wee titbit here and a wee titbit there, so you were basically flying by the seat of your pants. You got the impression that neither he nor his backroom staff had ever watched the opposition because they gave you absolutely no detail about the players you were about to face. Brown would remain manager until 1971 but I don't know how he did it.

The biggest problem we had as Scotland players was that we didn't have any worthwhile guidance. We didn't have a tactician who could suss out the opposition and talk about how we could counter them and give them problems. If you don't have that type of preparation, and things start to go against you on the park, the cracks appear and everything begins to disintegrate. Sir Alf Ramsey, the England manager when I was a Scotland player, was a deep thinker about the game and would send his teams out well briefed and well prepared. We also played against West Germany, with Franz Beckenbauer, and you could see that they were tactically aware. Back at club level, with Celtic, Jock Stein was a master at sending us out fully prepared after having gone through the strengths and weaknesses of the opposition with a fine-tooth comb, so we all knew exactly what our roles were, what we had to do and when we had to do it.

So when we went down to England in April 1967 to face the world champions at Wembley we were pretty much a rudderless ship. We got next to no help from the management so it was up to the players to work things out for ourselves. It helped us that we knew all about the opposition: the England team that took the field at Wembley that Saturday afternoon was exactly the same as the one that had won the World Cup nine months previously, except that Jimmy Greaves was in the forward line in place of Roger Hunt. So we knew how they were going to play. This was Bobby Brown's first match in charge of Scotland and his team talk was, 'Well, boys, you're representing Scotland. Go out there and do your best.' So we had our own team talk, among ourselves, in the dressing room before the match while Bobby Brown was prancing around in the background. It also helped that we had players who were ideal in terms of keeping the ball, such as Jim Baxter, and players around him who were running and supporting him, such as wee Bremner and Denis, who would drop off the forward line to link up with Baxter or with Bremner. Eddie McCreadie of Chelsea was overlapping on the left and I was doing the same thing on the right; I always switched to right-back when Eddie was in the team.

Matches with England were hate matches. Once the game was over we would happily have a drink with the English guys but on the park there was no messing about: if you got the chance to split someone in two that is exactly what you did – fairly, of course . . . So we were motivated less by playing the world champions than by playing England, the Auld Enemy, because the annual contest with them was always fierce, regardless of achievements in World Cups. At one point early in the match I went on an overlap and Ray Wilson, who was the England left-back, went right over the top of the ball, his stud went into the top of my instep and the bone was bruised. I was sitting on the English goal-line getting treatment when Denis Law scored our first goal. I got straight up and ran after him; I never felt the injury as soon as I saw that goal go in. Later in the game I could feel that the instep was a wee bit iffy but it didn't affect my running or tackling.

Baxter was the main man that day at Wembley; as soon as we got the ball we were looking for him. We knew that he could hold it and wouldn't give it away. Against that England team, it was vital either to make a telling pass or to keep possession, and that's what we did on the day. I can't remember Baxter misplacing a pass once that afternoon. He was always the outlet but he insisted you get the ball to his feet: if you put the ball ten yards in front of Jim Baxter you could forget about it, he would refuse to run after it. The only real drawback with Jim that day was that he wanted to take the mickey out of the English. Denis Law wanted to do the opposite: he wanted to give the English a hammering and our team was equipped to do that. Denis had been getting a lot of stick from the English players at Manchester United because he played for Scotland, especially after England had won the World Cup, so when we went in front, Denis wanted to rub salt in the wound.

We could have scored five or six that day. Gordon Banks, the England goalkeeper, made some fantastic saves. At one point, Denis Law chipped him and it looked a certain goal because Banks had come well off his line, but Banks arched his back in mid-air, reached behind him and tipped the ball away. I still don't understand how he got up in the air to palm the ball away. It was a better save than the one he made low on his line from Pele in the 1970 World Cup finals, which has been celebrated ever since. Banks' excellence and Baxter's easy-oasy approach meant that as we reached the final 25 minutes of the match we were still only 1–0 up even though we had dominated the game. Baxter still wanted to show off instead of looking to score more goals. He wanted to knock the ball around, have the English players chasing around and make them look silly. Denis wanted to push forward and have a real go at them and maybe get another two or three goals. Billy Bremner tried to get Baxter to knuckle down but his words went in one ear and out of the other. There wasn't much we could do about it because he was the playmaker and everything had to go through him. It was frustrating for us, his team-mates, because that is the sort of thing you do in the final five minutes, not when there are 25 minutes to go. Close to the end, Baxter was doing a wee bit of keepy-uppy to try and embarrass the English even more and we nearly counted the cost of that, despite Bobby Lennox putting us 2–0 ahead.

Jackie Charlton, the England centre-half, had broken his toe after quarter of an hour of the match when he had clattered into Bobby Lennox, who emerged from that encounter with a hole in his knee. Bobby could play on but Charlton was struggling. At that time, though, no substitutes were allowed, so Jackie Charlton had to play on at centre-forward, as a target man, and they kept firing in high balls for Jackie Charlton to get up and nod them in the direction of our goal. That is how they got their opening goal, making it 2–1 to us with five minutes remaining. All of a sudden, instead of being on easy street, home alone, we found ourselves under pressure. After Baxter had slowed the game down to walking pace, we now had to step up the tempo again and that's not easy: once you lower the pace of a game it is very difficult to pick it up again. In the final five minutes we were hanging on by our fingernails and although we managed to get a third through Jim McCalliog to make it 3–1, Geoff Hurst, the English centre-forward, scored with a header right at the death and with us 3–2 ahead we had to claw our way through the nervy final stages. It should never have been like that; we should have had the game sewn up comfortably long before then, so superior were we to the English that day. They had gone nineteen matches unbeaten but we had the satisfaction of becoming the first country to beat them since they had won the World Cup.

Denis was raging at Baxter after the game because we had actually put more pressure on oursleves than England had. Denis had been screaming at Baxter to get moving and speed up the game and I agreed with Denis. We were only 1–0 up when he started messing about and if we had gone for the throat and made it 3–0 or 4–0, as we should have done, anything could have happened after that. We could easily have subjected the English to a record defeat. I had made two crashing tackles, fair tackles, on Jimmy Greaves in the opening ten minutes. I had really hit him hard because he was playing wide, in between the central defenders and me. That brought me a great compliment from Jock Stein after the game. He said, 'A great part of that victory was due to you because of the two tackles you made on Greaves because after that I never saw him. The start of the game was one of the most important things in getting the victory and you really rattled him because of the way you took the ball away from him.'

That England team, although massively inferior to us on the day, was a magnificent one. Bobby Moore, at the back, could read the game and fill in gaps in defence and make last-gasp tackles. He was the perfect foil for big Jackie Charlton in much the same way as, at Celtic, John Clark was for Billy McNeill. George Cohen and Ray Wilson were fine full-backs, Alan Ball and Nobby Stiles were tireless in midfield and they had very good forwards in Martin Peters, Geoff Hurst and Bobby Charlton. Our team, though, was more than a match for them in terms of talent. Ronnie Simpson was winning his first cap at the age of 36 and Willie Wallace and Bobby Lennox were my other Celtic team-mates. John Greig and Ronnie McKinnon of Rangers made it six Old Firm players in the team. The England-based Scots – Jim McCalliog, Billy Bremner, Eddie McCreadie and Denis Law – were all top-class players. The English always thought they were superior and that because the Celtic and Rangers players did their stuff in the Scottish League we weren't in the same class as them. Well, with more than half of that team composed of Old Firm players we stripped them of the unbeaten record they had maintained since their victory over West Germany in July of the previous year – so our League can't have been bad, can it? I think they may have underestimated us before the match but they found out, on the day, how good we were. We had 70 per cent of the ball – it is just a shame that we failed to convert that possession into chances.

Bobby Brown's after-match comment in the dressing room was, 'Tonight, boys, London belongs to you.' We attended the post-match dinner at the Café Royal and the English guys were away in a corner sulking at having been thoroughly outclassed. We, on the other hand, were ready to celebrate and were very glad to accept an invitation to a party in the nearby Shaftesbury Theatre that was being held to celebrate the 10,000th performance of *The Mousetrap*, the Agatha Christie play. A representative of the theatre had suggested that we go up to the theatre later on and join the party. So at about ten o'clock we ambled up there. The injury I had suffered during the match had stiffened up and I was hirpling about. It was a dull ache, like toothache, and it was a worry with the European Cup final less than six weeks away, but I was determined that it wouldn't stop me celebrating.

We had been drinking almost since the final whistle and by late in the evening most of us were suitably merry but Billy Bremner was absolutely legless and he was still downing the drinks as we partied on in this wee private bar inside the Shaftesbury Theatre. Then who bowls in but Cilla Black, the pop singer, and Frankie Howerd, a camp comedian who had a very popular television show at the time. As Cilla Black went up to talk to wee Bremner, the rest of us said, 'Oh no . . .' She said to him, 'Oh, Billy, what a wonderful day for you and your team, to have beaten the world champions. Your fans must be so happy for you and your players must feel so good.' Bremner, whose eyes were rolling in his head by this time, responded, 'You must be the worst fucking singer I've ever heard in my life.' So Frankie Howerd, all agitated, steps in and says, 'Now, Billy, Billy, Billy, that's not a very nice thing to say.' Bremner swayed back, then forward, tried to focus on Howerd and said, 'And you must be the biggest fucking poofter I've ever seen in my life.' We were all falling about the place and the two of them walked out. Our carousing carried on for several more hours and by the end of the evening I was feeling no pain, from my injury or otherwise. Fortunately, within a week the knock had cleared up completely.

All four of the home nations, at that time, had extremely good players. Scotland and England would normally beat Northern Ireland and Wales but could sometimes come a cropper. The Irish had in their team top-class players such as George Best, Pat Jennings, the goalkeeper, and Derek Dougan, the centre-forward. We went to play the Irish in Belfast in late 1967 and I was at right-back, which meant I was directly opposed to Bestie, who was playing as a left winger. I couldn't get near him; it was like trying to catch the wind. He gave me a real going-over in the first half and Ronnie Simpson, who was in goal, made some great saves. So at half-time Bobby Brown said to me, 'What are we going to do?' I was thinking to myself, 'Well, you're the manager . . .' So I took on the manager's role as he stood there, wondering what to do, and I said, 'The first thing we will need to do is cut out the supply to him. So we'll need to tighten up in the middle of the park and stop them feeding him. In the meantime, I'll get as tight to him as I can. If he doesn't get the ball to his feet there is nothing he can do. So if there is anything stuck inside me, one of the centre-backs can come out and cut it out.' That was the plan for the second half but when we went out Bestie had switched to the right-hand side. Eddie McCreadie was playing left-back so I just waved across and said, 'All the best, Eddie.' Best proceeded to give him a roasting and they beat us 1–0 but it was 1–0 going on five.

I always liked to be picked for Scotland squads: it was an honour, and even more of an honour actually to play. Nevertheless, big Jock talked me into withdrawing from seven or eight international squads when Celtic had key games coming. If there was an international on a Wednesday and Celtic had a key game on the Saturday, he would say, 'You don't want to bother playing there.' He would also make it worth my while not to turn up for Scotland. If you played for Scotland, or were in the squad, you would receive an international fee from the SFA. If I pulled out of a Scotland squad, at Jock's behest, he would make sure that I still received the amount due – but in cash from Celtic. Not only that but, unlike the international fee from the SFA, the substitute one from Celtic would be tax-free, which was quite a boon. My first international fee, in 1966, had been £40 – a fair sum, the equivalent of a week's wages from Celtic. But it took a while to come through from the SFA, approximately two months after the match whereas when Celtic paid me my international match fee in lieu I received it the following week. So you could say that Jock had a nice bonus system in place for anyone whom he wished to miss an international; it made for quite an incentive for us to pull out of Scotland matches as and when Jock required.

If there was a Scotland match on the horizon and it was one that Jock wanted you to miss, he would come up to you stealthily, put his hand on your shoulder and say, very persuasively, 'Now, I'll leave it up to yourself but we've got an important game on Saturday and it is up to you whether you want to pull out of the Scotland match. If you do, I'll phone the manager and you will get your fee from us.' So you would think about it and if Scotland were playing against a country that was not going to present too big a challenge, you would pull out. One such occasion was a World Cup qualifier with Cyprus in Nicosia in December 1968, a match in which nobody wished to play because it was a long way to travel simply to give the locals a hammering. Jock told me I didn't want to be going to Cyprus simply to participate in a walkover so I withdrew from the Scotland squad for that one. The Scandinavian nations were also pretty poor – it is different today – and I pulled out of a European Nations Cup qualifying match with Denmark at Hampden in December 1970. So I was pulling out of matches against teams that I knew that we were going to beat; big Jock would phone Bobby Brown and tell him I had a groin strain or whatever. If I had not done that I could have had another seven or eight caps. Nobody ever questioned how you could fail to play for Scotland on a Wednesday but take the field, looking fully fit, for your club side on a Saturday. All the Celtic players did the same thing but if four or five of us were picked for a Scotland squad, then two would drop out and three would play; then, the next time, a different two would drop out. We had a bit of a rota system going for pulling out of international matches.

My first loyalty was to Celtic so I always had to do what was best for Celtic. The Scotland games from which I withdrew were mainly friendly matches or minor qualifying matches. I always made the big Home International matches and the important qualifying matches for the World Cup or European Nations Cup. Sometimes, big Jock would approach me and ask me if I had thought about dropping out of a squad for a Scotland match and I would tell him that it was a game in which I wanted to play. That was fine; he would have no problem with that. It wasn't hard to choose the matches in which I wanted to play: you could always tell which Scotland matches were the key ones and which could be missed to give you the chance to concentrate on Celtic and on winning your match bonus on the Saturday.

This was in the era before the Tartan Army began to win a reputation as friendly football supporters who will support their team even as it suffers the most awful results. At the time I was playing for Scotland, support for the international team was quite different. Nowadays, people from all over the country attend Scotland matches at home and abroad but in the '60s and early '70s the Scotland support would be 75 per cent Rangers supporters. You didn't have Scotland supporters travelling from the likes of Aberdeen and the Highlands; it was mainly Glasgow punters, but there weren't many Celtic supporters who went to Scotland games. There were good reasons why people did not travel from afar to see Scotland play at Hampden: they had less money so they were less able to travel long distances to see matches. The road system was also less well developed, so it was quite difficult to get from one end of the country to the other.

Jimmy Johnstone suffered quite seriously from the concentration of Rangers supporters in Scotland crowds. He was given dog's abuse by them because they thought that Willie Henderson should have been playing in his place. They would even boo wee Jinky despite the fact that he always played well for Scotland. It was totally unfair and he became fed up with it, as would anyone who was turning on the magic but getting a hard time from his own supporters. How humiliating is that? I felt for him when I was playing for Scotland and heard the abuse that was flooding down the terraces in Jimmy's direction. I would discuss it with the Rangers players in the team and they would all agree that it was awful, but there was nothing that any of us could do. If the supporters decide to give a player a hard time, there is little that his team-mates can do about it. Jimmy was sickened by it. I can remember him telling Jock, on numerous occasions, far more often than me, 'Phone the manager, say I'm injured and pull me out.'

I didn't experience anything like that because the Rangers player with whom I was vying for the left-back position was Davie Provan and even the Rangers supporters acknowledged that Davie Provan wasn't the greatest player in the world. For Scotland teams at that time, there was always a bias towards picking Rangers players. Then the positions where the Rangers players failed to fit the bill would be filled by Celtic players. The rest of the team would be Anglos. Remember, three ex-Rangers players held the post of Scotland manager from the early '60s until the early '70s. Picking Glasgow players was also believed to draw a larger crowd to the game, particularly if it was one of the less glamorous fixtures.

There were some excellent players available to Scotland and I was happy to receive some personal acclaim in an era when we were blessed with numerous top talents. The European press would pick a world eleven and a European eleven every year and I was pleased to be picked for the world eleven twice and for the European eleven three times. Those were newspaper teams but I was also picked to play in a European eleven in a testimonial match in Lisbon for Mario Coluna, a tremendous left-sided midfield player for Benfica and Portugal. It was a sparkling occasion and the Stadium of Light was packed because he had given great service to Benfica as a player and as their club captain. Bestie played that night, as did Bobby Moore, Geoff Hurst and Martin Peters. The rest of the team was composed of Spanish and Italian players. It was nice to get recognition like that because Scotland failed to qualify for the finals of the World Cup or the European Nations Cup, despite having several world-class players. Of those, Jim Baxter, at his best, was certainly fit to strut alongside any of the greatest global talents, as was Jimmy Johnstone. Wee Billy Bremner could play in any company as could Denis Law, who had been European Footballer of the Year. Those players were indisputably world class but we had numerous others who were not far short of their level, if short of it at all.

Tam Reid was chairman of Partick Thistle and an earthy president of the SFA. 'Tell them to go and fuck off if they're bothering you,' he would say to us. He was good, as was Tommy Younger, who was a Hibs director. Others were less impressive. On any trip abroad, the team hotel would be swarming with blazered SFA councillors on a junket, getting stuck into the booze. These councillors sat on the SFA Council and solemnly laid down the law for the Scottish game; they would also be on the selection committee that picked the pool of players for the Scottish national team. Some of them were on the committee of a South of Scotland League club or Highland League club, or from schools football or Junior football, and yet they would be making key decisions that would affect the national game at top level.

A 1–1 draw with England at Hampden Park in early 1968 scuppered our chances of reaching the finals of that year's European Nations Cup in Italy. The Home Internationals of 1966–67 and 1967–68 had doubled up as a qualifying section for the final stages of the European Nations Cup and we had gone top of the group after our 3–2 victory over the English at Wembley in April 1967, a victory that made us British champions for 1966–67. The 1–0 defeat in Belfast later that year, though, had been a severe setback, allowing the English to regain top spot in the European Nations Cup qualifying group, and the English had come to Glasgow for our final fixture in February 1968 requiring just one point to go forward at our expense. A victory would have seen us eliminate them but it was not to be. We drew 1–1 and missed out on the European finals.

We were confronted with another difficult group when the draw was made for the qualifying stages of the 1970 World Cup. We found ourselves in the same group as West Germany, who had been World Cup finalists in 1966, Austria and Cyprus. We put thirteen goals past Cyprus to defeat them home and away, drew 1–1 at home with the Germans and defeated the Austrians 2–1 at Hampden. It wasn't a bad record but it meant that when we travelled to Hamburg to play West Germany in October 1969 we had to win to have a good chance of securing a place in the 1970 World Cup finals. If we beat the Germans we would then need only a draw against Austria in Vienna. A draw in Hamburg would keep our hopes of qualification alive but a defeat would knock us out. It was a vitally important match for Scotland but I was unaware just how crucial those 90 minutes would be for me. The match with West Germany would prove to be the turning point in my football career: not so much at international level but when I returned to club football with Celtic afterwards.

Jimmy Johnstone got us off to a great start when he clipped the ball over Sepp Maier, the German goalkeeper, to put us in the lead. The Germans hit back but Alan Gilzean equalised for us to make it 2–2 midway through the second half and we went on to dominate the game, despite Jim Herriot, who was in goal for us that evening, having a total nightmare. We had come close to getting the third goal that might just have seen us win when, instead, Reinhard Libuda put the Germans 3–2 ahead with only nine minutes remaining. We continued to go forward, seeking an equaliser, and I was about 25 yards out, just about to hit a shot, when Helmut Haller, the Germans' outside-left, came in and halved me with a flying tackle. He never went near the ball; he just took my legs away from me. I was raging because I had been in my favourite position, just outside the 'D', and ready to hit one from a part of the park from which I scored a lot of goals. Anything could have happened if I had had the chance to hit that. We were all desperate to get an equaliser and a goal for us would have had them rocking; we had the initiative at that stage even though they had scored their third goal during what had been a good spell for us.

It might have been OK if the referee had given us a free kick; we could then have had a pop at goal but no, the referee did not even award us a foul though Haller's offence was as clear as day. That didn't help my mood as I felt a rush of blood to the head in my anger at the incident. I got up, ran after Haller, who was around ten yards away, and, in utter frustration, lashed out at him with a kick. He went down as if he was dead. The person who retaliates, of course, is always sent off; Haller, the instigator, was not even spoken to by the referee. As soon as he saw me being sent off, he stopped rolling about and got up on his feet. There had been nothing wrong with him. It was the first time in my career I had been sent off but you can only take so much punishment before retaliating.

After I was dismissed by the referee, I went into the dugout, even though I was supposed to go straight to the dressing room. I sat in the dugout and the referee never did anything. With about two or three minutes to go, Bobby Brown told the substitutes and myself that it would be a good idea to go to the dressing rooms, which were away down in one corner of the ground. As we walked along the track, the German fans started hurling bottles towards us from the terracing. So we jogged on to the park and trotted along the edge of the park, while the game was going on, to get away from them. Once we reached the corner flag, we were confronted with a ramp that led up to the dressing rooms and that made us once again an easy target for the fans, who began hurling bottles at us as we tried to go up. The police weren't bothering themselves to do anything to help us. Fortunately, no one was hurt seriously; the sending off was to do me more harm than any of those bottles. That dismissal in Hamburg was to become a watershed in my Celtic career, even though it had been sustained whilst wearing the dark blue of Scotland.

The Germans got the result they needed – it stayed at 3–2. They were a very skilful side. Franz Beckenbauer was a majestic player. Uwe Seeler and Gerd Muller, both of whom played against us in Hamburg, were of identical build: small, stocky strikers who would sniff out and snap up any chance going inside the penalty area and could score in quite ingenious ways. I was up against Libuda, the right winger, that night and he was a flying machine. It was hard work playing against him. Haller himself, who played with Bologna in Italy, was a great player as were Sepp Maier, the goalkeeper, and Berti Vogts, the terrier of the side. They already had the nucleus of the team that would reach the semi-finals of the 1970 World Cup, win the European Nations Cup in 1972 and the World Cup in 1974. It shows you how good we were that we were able to hold our own against them and get within an inch of beating them and eliminating them from the World Cup. If we had had that wee bit of extra organisation and tactical awareness from the backroom staff we could probably have been even better as a team.

I was back in the Scotland team for the 0–0 draw with England at Hampden in the spring of 1970 but absented myself from the home match with Denmark in November of that year, which was the first qualifying match for the 1972 European Nations Cup finals and resulted in a 1–0 victory over the Danes. I rejoined the squad for the next European Nations Cup qualifying match, against Belgium in Liege in February 1971. Archie Gemmill and Tony Green made their debuts for Scotland that day but we lost 3–0. It was to be my final appearance for my country. I had won eighteen caps.

There was never anything wrong with the team spirit or the fitness of the Scotland players but five years on from my debut, there remained a lack of leadership and an absence of proper, thorough preparation from the managerial side. It was far from ideal but I still wanted to play for Scotland and I always hoped that things would get better. They never really did. Scotland matches added welcome variety to the season in the same way as European Cup fixtures did at club level, but being with Scotland was like being at a holiday camp: discipline was a wee bit lax. If a player turned up a quarter of an hour late for his dinner, nobody turned a hair. Now that may sound like a little thing but if several small lapses of discipline like that are overlooked it tends to diminish the manager's authority. A general feeling of slackness subconsciously affects the players, so that if you go out on the park and things are not happening for you, you say to yourself: ach well, if it happens it happens; if it doesn't happen, it doesn't happen. But if you have a disciplinarian manager keeping a tight rein on things it can be a different ball game. With Scotland, the discipline wasn't as strict as with Celtic, possibly because the managers didn't have the same strength of character as big Jock. The Scotland managers may also have been thinking that, as we weren't their players, they could not be too hard on us.

We knew that we players had to sort out for ourselves any organisation on the park. It didn't always work but we always gave it our best shot. There was nothing better than a Scotland victory, especially at Hampden or Wembley, in front of 100,000-plus crowds, and I felt a real sense of national pride on those occasions. Once you put on that Scotland jersey, you wanted to go out there and go for it. I never went out to play for Scotland and treated it lightly. I may have absented myself from the squad a few times when we were playing minor matches but when I turned up to play for my country I was always determined to do my very best. The rest of the lads were the same: we all wanted to win for Scotland and never took opponents lightly. But we needed that little bit of extra help from the management and it was never forthcoming.

7. PARTING SHOTS

Teamwork won the European Cup for Celtic but shortly after the Lisbon victory I had reason to question Jock Stein's repeated stressing of the importance of the team ethic. That was as the result of a financial matter that concerned me in the summer of that European Cup-winning year of 1967. Before I was married, I went out on a few dates with big Jock's secretary and I put her on the spot and asked her what Billy McNeill was earning because I had a sneaking feeling that it was more than the rest of us. She answered, 'Ten pounds a week more than you.' That meant that Billy's weekly earnings were 25 per cent greater than those of the rest of us: we were getting £40 and he was getting £50.

I went in to see big Jock. 'Boss,' I said, 'you're always telling us it's a team game, that no one player is better than the other, that we've all got to play for each other and that we are all equal. So how come there is a player playing in the team that is getting ten quid a week more?' big Jock responded, 'How do you know that?' I said, 'I just found out by accident. I think we should all get the same money.' Jock said, 'Aye, but he's got responsibilities. He's captain.' 'Well,' I said, 'make me captain and give me an extra tenner.' Jock said, 'Oh, no, no, no. I can't do that.' Mine was a valid point because we were all, really, captains on the park; we would all lambast each other if necessary.

After my meeting with big Jock I went back to the dressing room and told the boys that Caesar was getting a tenner a week more than us. They weren't too happy about it. Still, as a result of my action, we all got a fiver a week rise at the beginning of the 1967–68 season. I then found out – from the same source as before, Jock's secretary – that Billy had also been given an extra fiver a week, so he was still getting a tenner a week more than the rest of us. I had hoped that we would get another tenner a week to bring us up to the same level. I would have to say that Billy did earn his money: we may all have had the potential to be captain but Billy was the man who actually did hold that position and he was a good captain. I imagine his extra responsibilities would have included meetings before matches with big Jock, at which, I expect, big Jock would tell Billy what he wanted from the players in that particular match and would make it clear that it was for Billy to keep the players on their toes.

That episode, however, did nothing to upset the equilibrium of the dressing room. We all took too much pride in our performance to let something like that upset us. It was important but it wasn't *that* important because nearly every week we were getting win bonuses and we felt fairly comfortable financially. Our basic wage was more than enough to live on and the bonuses were our spending money. I was paying around £30 per month on a mortgage of £2,800. The price of the house in Kirkintilloch had been £4,800 and I had put £1,000 of my savings down as a deposit and been given a £1,000 interest-free loan by Celtic. I did not blame Billy at all for accepting a deal that gave him £10 extra; whatever you can get in the game of football, you take.

I had had to do all the negotiating over the wages by myself: I didn't know what an agent was. It would not have mattered, anyway, because if you had employed an agent and they had approached big Jock to ask him to change your contract, I know exactly what he would have said: two words, the second of which would have been 'off'.

The Lisbon Lions started a match together on only five further occasions after we had won the European Cup in May 1967. Four of those were in the League Cup at the very beginning of the 1967–68 season; the other was the first leg of our first round European Cup tie with Dynamo Kiev at Celtic Park on 20 September 1967. That would prove to be the last time we began a game together, although on one further occasion, in a match at Motherwell in early 1968, we ended the match together after John Hughes had been substituted by Stevie Chalmers, reuniting the eleven who had triumphed in Lisbon. It had been a great side, one that could have held its own against any team in the world, then or since. We would have been a match for the Ajax of Johan Cruyff, the Bayern Munich of Franz Beckenbauer, the Milan of Marco van Basten; the Real Madrid of Zinedine Zidane. We possessed tremendous fitness, our teamwork was close to flawless and our all-round ability in defence and midfield provided a platform for attacking players who could score goals in any company. We did not need to fear anybody. We could play against any side in the world and not have to worry about it, provided everybody in our team played to the best of his ability. I have never seen a club side that bettered ours.

Jimmy Johnstone was the man who made the difference between a good side and a great side. Wee Jinky was our key man, a specialist in cracking the combination that would open up the back four of any opposition, especially when we were up against defensive sides who tried to hit you on the break. A wave of confidence would surge through our team every time we got the ball to wee Jinky's feet. He scored a number of goals but, even more importantly, he laid on numerous chances for everybody else. He did so much damage to defences: he'd go past defenders, bring the ball back and go past them again, bring it back and go past them for a third time. The only way they could stop Jimmy was to have a go at him. He could deal with that – he was brave and he could give it out too, when necessary.

You didn't knock the ball into space for wee Jinky; you had to give it to him at his feet. He didn't race down the touchline: he would check, come back and then run straight at defenders. He would ease past one defender so others would be pulled out from the centre to deal with him, and that would leave space inside the penalty area for guys like Stevie Chalmers and Bobby Lennox. Sometimes, Jimmy did hold on to the ball for too long and the space in the middle would be closed off. Jimmy would have turned back to beat one too many defenders and the guys in our side who had made runs would need to check and make another run. He could be a wee bit frustrating at times, to us, but that would not bother those on the terraces; his ability was tremendous and he was great to watch. Bobby Lennox, on the opposite wing, was an excellent footballer but quite different from Jimmy. Bobby would very rarely try anything of which he was not capable. He relied on his pace, his vision, his running off the ball and his reading of situations. It brought him and the team numerous goals; he was a real players' player.

Jimmy could have played in any team in the world and would have been a star. He tends to be overlooked when lists of the world's greatest players are drawn up; other players of that era, such as George Best and Alfredo Di Stefano, are always listed, but I believe that is because they played in leagues that were supposedly of a higher calibre than the Scottish League. People outside Scotland think, wrongly, that playing in the Scottish League is like taking tea in the park. They will always think that, although many top continental and English clubs have come a cropper against Celtic both in my time as a player and in recent seasons.

I first played against George Best in a pre-season friendly in August 1966 when we defeated Manchester United 4–1 at Celtic Park. That was the Manchester United side that would win the Football League Championship in 1967, and we gave them a thrashing. George and I played against each other again, in another friendly, in Toronto, Canada, and twice in internationals between Scotland and Northern Ireland. I also played with him in Mario Coluna's testimonial match in Lisbon. Bestie was a better all-round player than Jinky but, for individual skill, Jinky was streets ahead. Jinky was much better at taking players on, going past them and making openings. Bestie could do the same thing but he wasn't as clever at it as wee Jinky although, like wee Jinky, he was brave and he could score goals and make goals. There was a lot more in Bestie's repertoire: he was good in the air; he would tackle. He was the best player that I played against directly in a competitive match. He was very similar to Di Stefano in the way he could see things happening but for pure ability there was nobody like wee Jinky and I have never seen anyone like him in the years since. At his best, he was unstoppable. In training he would keep trying to nutmeg me and he did it successfully quite a few times. He was allowed three and no more. I told him that if he nutmegged me more than three times he was fair game.

That friendly against Manchester United in Toronto was memorable for unusual reasons. The two clubs were billeted in the same top-notch hotel, the Royal York, and in a wee lane that ran behind the hotel sat an Irish restaurant called O'Malley's. Wee Bertie, myself, Billy McNeill and Wispy Wallace told Paddy Crerand that we would meet him and some Manchester United players in that restaurant for a bite of lunch on the day of the game, which had an evening kick-off. Paddy brought along Bestie and Nobby Stiles and Bestie said to us, 'Are we having a drink?' So we ordered seven half pints of lager, to keep things in check, bearing in mind that we had a game to play a few hours later. We then got in another seven half pints. Bestie downed his second half-pint and said that he had had enough lager – but then he said, 'Why don't we get some bottles of Mateus Rosé?' So we downed the contents of those and Bestie ordered some more. By then, it was about four o'clock in the afternoon and we were supposed to be in our beds, resting, in advance of the match. We made a nice wee pact with the Manchester United boys that we would just knock the ball about in the match; not do anything strenuous, such as tackling. They said they would pass the word around their players and we said we would do the same.

That night, I was facing Bestie: I was at left-back and he was on United's right wing. He got the ball in the opening couple of minutes and went past three of us as if he hadn't even seen that we were in his way. I said to him as he trotted back past me, 'Hey you, you little bastard, what about that arrangement we came to?' He said, 'I've never felt so fucking good in all my life.' They beat us and he tortured us that night; you would have thought he had never had a drink in his life. There were 35,000 at that match; little did they know how some of us had prepared for it.

We had come back for the 1967–68 season still on cloud nine after becoming the champions of Europe. We had only had a short break to recharge the batteries following our match against Real Madrid in the opening week of June. Within weeks, we were back at Celtic Park for pre-season training. I liked training although a lot of players didn't. Some people trained harder than others. Bertie Auld, for example, was one of the laziest trainers at the club and would do as little as possible but he turned it on on the park so it didn't matter. The thought of pre-season training, though, even for a good trainer like me, was always horrendous; probably worse than the actual thing because in the days beforehand you were tormented by the knowledge that you were going to get murdered. Jock Stein divided the squad into three groups: the heavy mob, the medium mob and the light mob. The heavy mob consisted of guys such as myself, Billy McNeill, big Yogi Hughes, Bobby Murdoch – all the taller and heavier players. During the close season I would normally put on between five and seven pounds, whereas wee Bobby Lennox or Stevie Chalmers would hardly have put on a pound. I would not have done a lot of exercise during the break except for one or two runs, just to get the wind going, shortly before pre-season training started. My feeling was that if I was going to be training hard and running for ten and a half months of the year, I was damned sure I would rest my legs as much as possible during the close season.

The heavy mob, in pre-season, got extra running and the lighter mob was spared the numerous laps and half laps that we were forced to do. We used to put on incontinence pants that came up past the waist and when you took them off after one of these pre-season training sessions, there was so much sweat gathered inside them that it was like throwing away a bucket of water. I would lose five or six pounds in a session at the start of pre-season training but, by the time I went home and had rehydrated, I would probably have lost only a pound or a pound and a half. The first few days of pre-season were real torture: every morning, as a result of the previous day's exertions, you would need a good half-hour of warming up just to get the stiffness out of your legs before you could do anything. After a week the stiffness subsided, although the muscles still ached a bit. After a couple of weeks you were back to normal. Those tough sessions would continue for the first week or ten days until we all got back to our fighting weights. Then the heavy mob would join in with the medium mob and the light mob.

We had wanted to carry on from where we had left off the previous season after winning the European Cup but unfortunately Dynamo Kiev knocked us out in the first round of the 1967–68 tournament. They played well to beat us 2–1 at Celtic Park then drew 1–1 with us over in Kiev. To go out in the first round of the European Cup, after winning it, was a wee bit humiliating. There was some consolation for us in that we would be contesting the World Club Championship, which many people saw as being an even bigger trophy than the European Cup. It was a contest that had been created to see which was the greatest club team in the world. It was played between the champions of Europe and the champions of South America and in 1967 that meant we would be facing Racing Club of Argentina. The first leg was moved to Hampden Park to accommodate the huge crowd that wanted to see the match; it was televised live throughout Europe and South America and the British prime minister, Harold Wilson, made a point of attending. The importance of the World Club Championship can be gauged from the fact that we were on a bonus of £1,500 to win it – the same sum as we had received for winning the European Cup.

Jock had done his homework and he knew that the players of Racing Club were very, very cynical. Sir Alf Ramsey had been right when, at the 1966 World Cup, he had called the Argentinians 'animals'. Jock told us that Racing Club would slow the game down as often as possible, stop us playing and prevent us stringing passes together and building up the game. We knew that if we were allowed to play we would beat them, but they never allowed us to play. In the first game, we could never string more than three passes together before they would concede a free kick to break up our rhythm. They would bodycheck you, chop you – whatever it took to stop you. They would jog past you, when the ball was nowhere near, and give you a tap on the ankle or a dig in the ribs. Our game was all about stringing passes together so their tactics had a serious effect on our attempts to get the game moving in our direction. We just couldn't get the game flowing long enough to cause them a lot of problems but we did end up winning 1–0, thanks to a header from Billy McNeill.

The same thing happened out in Buenos Aires, even though they were at home. We even lost our goalkeeper, Ronnie Simpson, who was struck on the head by a missile before the match and could not participate. I opened the scoring with a penalty kick but the match ended at 2–1 to them, making it 2–2 on aggregate, and the tie then went to a third game. Unfortunately, away goals did not count, otherwise we would have been the World Club Champions. Instead, the tie would go to a play-off in Montevideo, Uruguay, three days after the match in Argentina. It was in that third match that our frustration finally boiled over. It developed into nothing more than a kicking match. The players of Racing were evil and we were not in the mood to take any more after having been spat on, had our eyes gouged and hair pulled and been hacked at every opportunity in the previous two matches. It became a matter of who could kick whom the hardest. That is not very nice to say and it was not very nice to see.

Bob Kelly, the chairman, had wanted us to come back home from Buenos Aires after the second match because he had seen what had happened. He told Jock that he had witnessed two kicking matches and did not want to be taking players with broken legs back to Scotland on an aeroplane; it took almost a day to travel from South America, via Madrid and London, to Scotland. Big Jock, quite rightly, responded that if they allowed us to play football we would beat them; but Bob Kelly told him that we would not be allowed to play football, as had been shown in the previous two matches. Big Jock managed to bring him round to his way of thinking and we went ahead with the third match. We players also wanted to stay and show that we could beat them.

At the beginning of the third game, as soon as the match kicked off, their left winger, Raffo, came across and spat in the face of every defender. After that, we were looking to hit him hard, but fairly, in a tackle but every time he was threatened by a tackle, he pulled out of it. So he was the guy that I kicked in the bollocks with about twenty minutes to go. I have never seen it on videotape but they tell me it is quite comical. The referee, Rodolfo Osorio, a Paraguayan, missed that but he did not miss several other incidents: we had four men dismissed and two Racing players suffered the same punishment. Osorio did lose control of the game at various stages, and there were, on occasion, Uruguayan police on the pitch with their swords drawn. At the end, Osorio made Bertie Auld the fourth man in our team to be sent off but Bertie refused to leave the field. Osorio then restarted the match with a free kick to Celtic; he was having to award so many free kicks that he was probably confused by the time the match had reached those dying minutes. Racing won the match 1–0, but none of the three matches had a lot to do with deciding which was the best club football side in the world.

We had been due to receive a League Cup final-winning bonus of £250 for beating Dundee 5–3 shortly before we had flown out to Argentina but the chairman decided that he would withhold that money. He announced that every Celtic player had been fined their League Cup final bonus and that the money was going to go to charity. I suppose it was a good public relations exercise by the club to try to remove some of the tarnish from what had happened; Bob Kelly intended to show the world that we weren't the bad guys we were supposed to be and at the same time show the football authorities how seriously he, as chairman of Celtic, was taking the matter: for Celtic's reputation and the reputation of football, the players had to suffer for their conduct. I don't know whether the money did go to charity but I know we never got it. None of us was too happy about that fine because we had been goaded into doing things that we would never normally do by Racing Club's cynicism and their approach to the game. Nobody could have taken the treatment that we received without retaliating. We had also lost the chance of obtaining a large bonus for becoming World Club Champions, so it seemed unfair that we should also be stripped of the bonus that we had won fairly and squarely by beating Dundee in the League Cup final. At that time £250 was quite a bit of money, more than five times our basic weekly wage. I think Jock had some sympathy with the players' dissatisfaction but the chairman had dug his heels in and made his announce-ment to the world within hours of us landing back in Glasgow from South America, so there was little that could be done about it. We recovered well enough from that experience to go on to win our third successive League title in that 1967–68 season and in 1968–69 we won the second Treble in the club's history.

Tommy Callaghan, who had played against us for Dunfermline Athletic in the 1965 Scottish Cup final, had joined Celtic in November 1968 and had made a significant contribution to the capturing of the Treble. He had moved down from Fife and had bought a house in Bishopbriggs, close to me in Kirkintilloch and to Willie Wallace, who lived in Condorrat. Shortly after Tommy joined, we were due to go down to Seamill with the club so we arranged that Willie would drive Tommy and me to Celtic Park in his car to meet the team bus. Willie was ten minutes late in picking me up, later still in collecting Tommy, the traffic was heavy and by the time we arrived at the ground we were half an hour late and everyone was sitting on the bus. Jock, who was sitting in the front seat, said to Willie and me, 'You two – get on that bus!' and to Tommy, 'You – into my office!' Later, once we were at Seamill, Tommy told us Stein had said to him, 'The ink is not even dry on your contract yet. Don't you depend on those two bastards again! If we are meeting at a certain time, then you make sure you are here at that time, on the button, or you are out of the door.' Tommy had just bought a new house and was terrified at the prospect of making a quick exit from the club.

So we got to Seamill, where wee Bertie and I were rooming together, and next door Stein had Tommy sharing a room with Bobby Murdoch because Bobby at that time was reasonably stable. We were at Seamill for a short break, to undertake a couple of light training sessions, so I had taken down a bottle of vodka, half a dozen Cokes and half a dozen bottles of Guinness. After dinner big Jock said, 'You can have a pint but you must all be in your beds by half past ten.' So I knocked on Bobby and Tommy's door and asked them to come through for a wee snifter. Next thing, big Jock opens the door with his pass key. 'What do you lot think you are doing?' he says. Then he looks at Callaghan and roars, 'You again?' So he chased Tommy and Bobby back next door and he got all the bottles together, went into the bathroom and threw the lot into the bath. 'Get to your beds and get to sleep,' he said. 'I'll see you two in the morning at training.' He had no sooner gone than we knocked on the door of Tommy and Bobby's room. 'The big man's away – come on back in,' we said. I had checked the bath and the only thing that had smashed had been the empty Guinness bottles. The vodka bottle, the full Guinness bottles and the Cokes were all intact. So we were scooping up again and chatting away when we heard the pass key in the door again and there was big Jock with steam coming out of his ears. He said to

Tommy Callaghan, 'You – into my office first thing on Thursday morning, when we get back.' Tommy's face was whiter than a china cup. Once big Jock went away, wee Bertie and I were killing ourselves laughing because big Jock had never said anything to us – we were past it by that time. The next morning, the receptionist told us that Jock had been alerted to our antics by the chandelier in the lobby rattling every time we began moving about.

We were disappointed to go out of the European Cup in the quarter-finals to Milan in the spring of 1969. Pierino Prati scored an early goal in the second leg at Celtic Park to give Milan a 1–0 aggregate victory. Prati hit the ball in at the top of his run and, after that, trying to score was like hitting your head against a brick wall. That was a disaster because we had played so well in Milan to get a 0–0 draw. The goal had come from a mistake on our part when a throw-in from Jim Craig went to Billy McNeill who lost the ball to Prati. Other than that, Milan never made any chances but although we controlled the game we couldn't put the ball in the net. Still, they were a right good side and they went on to win the European Cup that year.

We set off in pursuit of the great trophy again at the beginning of the 1969–70 season, convinced we were good enough to land it for a second time. We got past Basle of Switzerland in the first round and were drawn against Benfica of Portugal in the second round, which was scheduled for November 1969. Between those two ties, my situation at Celtic Park changed radically. My sending-off in Scotland's World Cup qualifier in West Germany had altered my situation at Celtic in such a way that it would lead to my eventual departure from Celtic Park.

Jock Stein had been with the official SFA party that had attended the match in Hamburg and he was with us on the SFA plane on the way home to Scotland. We flew into Prestwick Airport on the Thursday morning after the match and then Jock took me, Billy McNeill and Jinky straight to the Marine Hotel in Troon, where the rest of the Celtic squad were preparing for the League Cup final against St Johnstone, which would take place two days later. Jock took the three of us through a testing training session and everything seemed normal to me; he did not even mention my dismissal in the Scotland match.

On the Saturday, I walked into the Celtic dressing room around 25 minutes before kick-off, which was my usual routine. I liked to get into the dressing room just long enough before the start to take my clothes off, put my strip and boots on and then go out for a warm-up. That way, I spent as little time as possible hanging around awaiting the action. Before I went into the dressing room, I would be at the main door, speaking to my cronies; we didn't have players' rooms in those days. Other players, such as Stevie Chalmers, liked to be sitting in the dressing room fully stripped and with their boots on an hour before kick-off but that was never my style. I had entered the dressing room and was just taking off my coat when Jim Kennedy, who had by then retired as a player and was working on the club's staff as a liaison officer, said, 'There is your ticket for the stand.' Jock Stein walked past me and never said a word; he did not even acknowledge that I was there. I looked over to my locker – all of the lockers at Hampden were numbered in relation to the team line-up – and saw that Davie Hay was getting changed at number three; he would clearly be playing at left-back that day. All the guys were looking at me. I said, 'Good luck, Davie,' and walked out of the dressing room. I felt terrible; completely drained. I could not believe what had happened.

It may have been a cup final but there was none of the palaver that surrounds the game of football nowadays, where, before the kick-off, they read out the players' first names slowly, one by one, so that the supporters can shout out their surnames and make a big hullabaloo about it. Instead, the teams were announced in a matter-of-fact fashion just a couple of minutes before every match began, even at a cup final. So everybody at the game had assumed that I would be playing until I went up into the stand. As I went to take my seat they were all looking at me as if to say, 'What's happened?' Some supporters asked me why I was not in the team. I said, 'I don't know. I couldn't tell you.' I can remember Bertie Auld opening the scoring for Celtic in the second minute but the rest of the game went by in a blur. Celtic hung on to beat St Johnstone 1–0 but I had left the ground long before the final whistle and wasn't there to see the trophy presented to the guys who had been my team-mates for so long. I was holding a party in my house that evening but I hardly had a drink. The events of the afternoon were going through my brain all the time. It was a hard one to take: being humiliated in front of your team-mates.

On the following morning I phoned Jock Stein at Celtic Park: he always held a press conference there on a Sunday morning. I said to him, 'Can you tell me why I was left out of the match yesterday?' He said, 'Not over the phone.' I said, 'Fine – I'll be there in twenty minutes.' I went in to see him and the press conference was breaking up just as I arrived. The journalists' heads were all turning but big Jock chased them out. He came up with a story that the chairman thought that, for the good image of Celtic and as a disciplinary action, I should be left out of the League Cup-final team after having been sent off in the international match. I said, 'Well, how come you didn't tell me that on Thursday or Friday or even up until midday on Saturday, before we left Troon? How do you think I feel after walking into the dressing room, expecting to play, and then getting handed a ticket by Jim Kennedy to go and watch the game from the stand? I wouldn't have liked to be told on Thursday or Friday that I was out of the team but I would have accepted it if the chairman did say that.' He said, 'I didn't need to tell you that I was leaving you out. I don't need to say anything to you.'

I only had Jock Stein's word that the chairman had said I should be omitted from the team to play St Johnstone. I will never know whether the chairman actually did say that or whether Jock Stein was using it as a convenient excuse to drop me. I told him that if we had been facing Rangers in the final I would have been in the team. He said, 'No, you wouldn't.' I said, 'Well, I think I would have.' It wasn't as if I had had a bad game in Germany: I had played, I thought, quite well and this story that I had been dropped on the word of the chairman did not really ring true to me because by then it was well known that it was Jock, not the chairman, who picked the team. The chairman had tried to pick the team early in Jock's career as manager but it had soon been established that it would be chosen solely by Jock, with no interference at board level. It seemed strange, then, that this policy had changed or been relaxed simply to drop me for the League Cup final. I believe that if Jock Stein had wanted to play me against St Johnstone, I would have been playing; but he simply thought he wouldn't need me.

He had never dropped me before but that was not the way to do it for the first time. A manager, I believe, should tell players they are not playing in advance of the match, and tell them why. So I told Jock that he had not given me a satisfactory answer about why I had been dropped and why he had humiliated me in the dressing room, and I asked him to put me on the transfer list. It was not a snap decision: I had thought about it long and hard overnight and had decided to make that request unless Jock came up with a reasonable explanation for what he had done. If he had given me a valid reason I could have accepted it. What upset me was not being dropped but the way it was done. After that episode, I still respected Jock Stein 100 per cent as a manager, but I had lost a lot of respect for him as a person.

I think Jock Stein had wanted to bring me down to earth: that was what was behind his dropping me. I and a few other guys, such as Bertie and Jinky, were a wee bit flamboyant; super-confident, shall we say. Jock had seen the white Jaguar and all the other daft things in which we were indulging and, although he had tolerated all of that for a long time, he had maybe just been trying to cut me down to size. He had different ways of treating players. Some he would coax in order to get the best out of them; others he would cajole. I was not one of those: I was one of the players on whom he had to use the rough edge of his tongue to get me geed up. I thought to myself, It's all right trying to bring somebody down a peg or two but to do it in that situation, 25 minutes before a Cup final, making the player take off his coat, put it back on again, embarrassed at being watched by his team-mates, and then having to go up to the stand . . . The entire episode was strange because I had had a smashing relationship with Jock until that happened.

At that time, you couldn't get away from a club unless they wanted you out of the door. There was no freedom of contract and Jean-Marc Bosman was a mere toddler somewhere in Belgium. I had signed a new three-year contract in 1967, after Lisbon, once the wages dispute had been settled, and you could not just walk out on a club. They could retain your registration for a long as it suited them. I was to remain on the transfer list for the remainder of my time at Celtic Park – two years and two months – and Jock told me that in all that time there was not one inquiry for me. I do not believe that. I had scored in a European Cup final and would score in a second one, in 1970, whilst on the transfer list; those two matches were broadcast across Europe and the European Cup final was the biggest club match of the season. I had been part of a very successful Celtic side that was well respected throughout Europe. I was still creating goals, still scoring goals from free kicks and penalty kicks and in that 1969–70 season alone I would score fifteen goals, making me, a full-back, one of the top scorers at the club. I was playing well and I was an international player. It was simply not possible that I could be placed on the transfer list and there would be no clubs at all interested in inquiring about my transfer or offering to buy me.

In fact, I know that Jock Stein was lying to me because at least two clubs were interested in the possibility of buying me and one of them, very temptingly, was Barcelona. Vic Buckingham, a distinguished-looking Englishman who had been manager of Fulham, West Bromwich Albion and Ajax Amsterdam, became manager of Barcelona in January 1970. A man committed to attacking football, Buckingham was a sophisticated tactician who had given Johan Cruyff his debut at Ajax and began the process that would take the Dutchman to Barcelona in the early '70s. Buckingham was engaged in regenerating Barcelona after a poor period and he was interested in having me join him at the Nou Camp. I would have been able to help him in his stated pursuit of bringing a more northern European mentality and playing style to the Spanish club – an exciting prospect. That January of 1970 I heard from a press guy that Barcelona had made inquiries of Celtic about me, and I decided to go and see big Jock. I couldn't tell him that I had heard of Barcelona's interest because, as soon as I said that, I would become complicit in what could be described as an illegal approach for my services; it would reveal to big Jock that I was being 'tapped'. Under SFA rules, I should have gone to big Jock and said, 'I have been approached by Barcelona.' If there were any illegal approaches for me I was supposed to tell my manager about them, but that would have been counter-productive because I was looking for a transfer and moving to Barcelona interested me. The fact that I was the one on the transfer list whose future was at stake did not matter – any transfer business had to be conducted first between the two clubs alone. If they agreed to do business, then, and only then, would they involve the player.

I was interested to see how Jock would react so I left it for a couple of days before I went to see him. By then he would have had time to digest the offer from Barcelona. If he said that he had not heard from any club concerning me, he would be telling porkies. I said, 'Boss, have there been any transfer inquiries about me yet?' He said, 'No, no, no, there have been no inquiries whatsoever.' He waved his big, left paw dismissively in my direction. He had obviously decided that even though I was on the transfer list I could still be of some use to him. Now, as well as knowing that Barcelona were interested in signing me, I also knew for a fact that Leicester City had put in an offer for me because I had been tapped by them. I had been asked if I would be interested in talking to Leicester City and had responded that I would be interested in talking to anybody. So then I said to Jock, 'Have there been no English clubs in for me, boss?' Again he swept his left hand through the air. 'No, no, no, no.' Frustratingly, there was nothing I could do. If I revealed that I knew anything about specific clubs inquiring after me, he would know that I had been tapped, and if I had discussed a transfer with any clubs other than Celtic then that would have been a breach of contract on my part. That was despite Jock Stein being one of the biggest users of the press to tap players in the history of football.

The whole thing was a game of duplicity. Jock knew that I was in his office because an offer was on the table and I had been tipped off about it but as long as he claimed that no offer had come in, I could not say that I knew otherwise. I had been approached by a pressman with regard to both potential moves but I cannot name him because he is still alive, still writing for the papers and still tapping players on behalf of football clubs.

It would have been something special to move to Barcelona; I could just see myself sitting on the Ramblas lapping up the café life. Not many British players, then or now, get the chance to play in continental Europe and, if they do, they do not always go to one of the great institutions of world football in a top league such as Spain's. We had played Barcelona at the Nou Camp in the Fairs Cup back in the mid-60s so I knew exactly how stupendous an arena it was. I was enticed by the thought of the Mediterranean lifestyle and of playing for a great club in a great stadium and I was also, of course, thinking to myself, *Muchos pesetas . . .* It was a sweet temptation and great to know that I was so highly rated that I had attracted interest from such a club, but there was absolutely nothing I could do to help make any potential move to Barcelona go ahead.

Tempting as a move to England or abroad was, I had never wanted to leave Celtic at all. I was with a club for which I wanted to play, one that was winning trophies and contesting European matches, and I was in the international team. You don't want to leave a set-up like that but if you get treated like a piece of dirt by the manager, you can't stand back and take it. Even when I had slapped in my transfer request I had been half-hoping he would say, 'No, we're not putting you on the transfer list.' But he had no reason to tell me that because he could block any move made for me anyway. So my being on the transfer list mattered not a jot as long as Jock Stein wished to keep me. If a club made an offer for me, he could simply say, 'We're not selling him.' The whole contractual and transfer system was weighted in favour of the clubs and it was seriously abused.

Being on the transfer list never affected my performance, my attitude or how Jock treated me in training. I did receive a winner's medal for that League Cup final but I did not want it: it was a medal for which I had not played. Two away League matches, at Aberdeen and Ayr, immediately followed the League Cup final with St Johnstone and after my confrontation with Jock Stein I was not selected for either. I did play against Clyde reserves at Celtic Park on the Saturday following the League Cup final and scored a screamer from 25 yards at a free kick. Sean Fallon was looking after the reserves that day so obviously Sean told Jock what I had done. He then brought me back into the first team for the League match with Hearts at Celtic Park, a fortnight after the

League Cup final, and that was because Benfica – Eusebio and all – were due at Celtic Park four days later for the first leg of our European Cup second-round tie with them, a match for which he knew he required my services.

On the Monday before the Benfica match, Jock told me, 'I'm playing you on Wednesday night.' I scored a screamer against Benfica in the opening seconds – Bertie Auld tapped a free kick, 25 yards out, sideways to me and I launched myself at the ball to send it streaking high into the top corner of the Benfica goal. I ran towards the Jungle terracing for their acclaim then turned in the direction of the dugout and made a gesture at Stein that he would not have been able to mistake. The thing was, he was still the winner. He had brought me back because he knew he needed me for the Benfica game and I had been fired up to show him what I could do. He knew I would be planning to do that because there was no one better at reading how players would react in any given situation. My opening goal helped him to get the result he wanted –we went on to win 3–0. I'm sure that when I knocked that one in against Benfica, big Jock would have had a chuckle to himself. He'd have been thinking, Oh, here we go, I've got him sorted out. He was clever but I still feel he hadn't been too clever in the way he had dealt with me over the League Cup final. Our relationship, following that episode, was never as strong as it had been before.

The good work of the first leg against Benfica was almost undone when we travelled to Lisbon for the return leg. We were very careless and gave away three goals, leaving the tie level at 3–3 after extra-time. Penalty shootouts had yet to be invented so the tie was settled on the toss of a coin and we won it. We should never have lost that 3–0 lead. The luck was with us in winning the toss of the coin but that ain't the way to emerge victorious from a European Cup tie. Fiorentina, the Italian champions, faced us in the quarter-finals and again we won 3–0 at home in the first leg. Bertie, myself and Willie Wallace got the ball midway inside their half when it was 3–0 to us and we made about twenty consecutive passes, just knocking it in a triangle. Next thing, I heard big Jock screaming in my ear from the Jungle side of the park. He had come out of the dugout and gone right round behind the goals and halfway round the track, and the angrier he got the more pronounced his limp became. He was telling us to get the ball moving. 'It is all right for you three,' he said, 'you can knock it around, but what if they get it into our half and someone who can't do that tries it and we lose a stupid goal?' Against Fiorentina in the return leg we made no mistakes and played cautiously, and although we lost the match 1–0 we went into the semis on a 3–1 aggregate.

That set up a tie with Leeds United, the champions of England, who thought they were invincible, though we never did. We would have been happy to come away from Elland Road a goal down from the first leg; instead, we came away 1–0 up, and were doing handstands. We had gone down to Leeds by rail – we had a private carriage on the train – and Lex McLean, the comedian, was in our carriage. He made the journey from Glasgow to Leeds feel like five minutes. He was non-stop, unbelievable. Wee Jinky was out of this world at Elland Road. Terry Cooper, the Leeds United left-back, must have nightmares every time someone mentions Jimmy Johnstone because he twisted Terry inside out in both legs of that semi. Norman Hunter, the Leeds centre-half, was shouting to Cooper, 'Kick him!' Cooper was shouting back, 'You come out and try to get a hold of the wee Scottish bastard to kick him!' Hunter came out and tried to stick it on Jimmy but the wee man just waltzed away from him.

We all played well against Leeds and in the second leg, in front of more than 136,000 fans at Hampden Park, we ran over the top of them and beat them 2–1. So much for England's invincibles. Those games against Leeds were two of the easiest I experienced in all the years I played in European football with Celtic. Leeds went away home with their tails between their legs and that result put their English media's gas at a peep. It had suited us that the English media had been brainwashing their own people – it made it easier for us because Leeds had so far to fall.

We faced Feyenoord of Holland in the European Cup final in Milan on 6 May 1970. After the high of the triumphs in Europe that season it was unbelievable how low we plunged in that final. It was a totally different situation to three years previously, when we had been underdogs against Inter. On that day in 1967, we had looked at Inter and thought they looked arrogant, but it was possibly more that they were very self-assured because they were playing in the best League in the world, we were playing in the Scottish League and they had already won the European Cup twice and were in their third final in four years. Perhaps the Feyenoord players looked at us in the same way and thought we looked arrogant. I don't think we were, but we were certainly confident. We had to be because you don't win all the European games, league matches and cups that we had unless you are very confident in your ability. On that night, though, we were maybe a wee bit over-confident.

I would say we probably underestimated Feyenoord as we were the hot favourites to win. We didn't go out thinking we were going to give them a going-over – they had too many good players for us to think that – but the team talk and the information that we got from Jock about Feyenoord weren't up to the usual high standard. He played it a bit too low-key, I felt, and never really built us up in the way you would expect before a European final.

I gave us a good advantage after half an hour with a goal that was very similar to a number of strikes with which I'd scored for Celtic down the years. I was about 25 yards out when Bobby Murdoch knocked the ball short for me to hit and all I had to do was get it on target and away from the goalkeeper. The referee, Concetto Lo Bello, a Sicilian, was positioned inside the penalty area in such a way that he had to move out of the way of my shot, and he certainly impeded the sight of the Feyenoord goalkeeper, Eddy Pieters Graafland, by running across his line of vision, but I wasn't caring too much about that at the time. Unfortunately, we lost a goal two or three minutes later when Rinus Israel headed the ball into our net. If we had held on to the lead for fifteen or twenty minutes and the game had settled down again, we would possibly have been OK but we lost the goal too quickly after scoring and that got them geed up again. They started knocking the ball about, which was something they could do well. They hardly ever wasted a pass; every one of them could use the ball, keep it, control it and pass it again. That was the basis of 'total football', a style of play that the Dutch were pioneering in the early 1970s in which every player was expected to be a pure footballer and, in theory, could slot into any position on the field when called upon to do so. Every Feyenoord player, from centre-back to centre-forward, was extremely comfortable on the ball and that gave them a real advantage. The secret of any good side is the ability to hold on to the ball and those Feyenoord players certainly knew that secret. Wim van Hanegem, who played on the right side of midfield and had a tremenduous left foot, never wasted a pass the whole night. Wim Jansen played on the left-hand side. Several of their players were Dutch internationals and would go on to help Holland reach the final at both the 1974 and 1978 World Cup tournaments so it was no disgrace to be beaten by them. It was a disgrace the way we played, though, because it was totally out of character for us. Normally we would control most of a match but we couldn't get the ball off Feyenoord and they ended up dominating the game.

If you start in second gear, it's hard to get into top gear and we never really changed up through the gears all night, even though at half-time Jock told us to pick up the game. It was all very well for him to say that, but to pick up the game, you've got to get the ball and we weren't winning the ball and holding on to it long enough to make passes and bring different players into passing movements. We would no sooner get the ball than we would give it away and it was hard to get it back off them. It was out of character because we didn't usually give the ball away lightly. Maybe that had something to do with the team selection. The team that lined up for the final was not quite the right one. Changes had been made that we thought shouldn't have been. George Connelly had played in midfield in the semi-finals against Leeds United, when we had been 4–3–3 and had clamped down hard on Leeds' much-touted midfield but he was made a substitute for the final, leaving only Bertie Auld and Bobby Murdoch in midfield in a 4–2–4. Feyenoord, though, were 4–3–3 for the final so they had an extra man in midfield and that may have allowed them more control over the match. Their strength was in midfield, with Jansen on the left and Van Hanegem on the right. Additionally, we had Jim Brogan in central defence, where George Connelly might have been a better selection if he was not playing in midfield.

Badly though we played, we were agonisingly close to the end of extra time when we lost the second goal. We were only minutes away from a replay and we could never have played so badly a second time. Also their second goal should not have stood – it should have been a penalty kick because Billy clearly handled the ball in the air before their striker, Ove Kindvall, stuck the ball in the net. As soon as Billy handled the ball, the referee should have given a penalty kick; whether he had the foresight to say that Kindvall was going to put the ball in the net, and therefore played the advantage, I don't know. There was a bit of time before the ball came down to Kindvall and Lo Bello let play go on, so if Kindvall had missed the chance, the referee would have had to award a goal kick to us. I suppose it was a brave decision by the referee to let Kindvall go on and finish it but it would have been interesting to see what would have happened if Kindvall had missed the chance or the ball had been saved. That is open to conjecture: he could not very well have allowed play to continue with Kindvall and then have awarded a penalty kick if Kindvall had missed his chance. There would have been uproar. He had to give a penalty kick either immediately or not at all. Once Kindvall had put the ball in the net, though, and the referee had awarded the goal, there was nothing we could do.

After the Feyenoord final people in Scotland began talking about us having been more interested in money than in the game, which was a load of rubbish because the only money we made other than what we got from Celtic was £50 a head for an exclusive team picture for one of the newspapers. Those stories arose after Jock was interviewed in the hours after the match, when he implied that our thoughts might not have been 100 per cent on the game. He did not say it directly, nor was he quoted as saying it, but he did imply that the players had become more interested in the commercial side of the game than in the football. That was a load of garbage. Whose mind would not be on a European Cup final if they were playing in it? You don't go into a European Cup final thinking about pound notes. We didn't even know what we would get for a bonus if we won – and we got absolutely nothing for being beaten. All we wanted to do was win the European Cup again.

Jock's team selection had been a surprise to us but he had picked the team that had won in 1967 and in 1970 he must have known what he was trying to do. We players must take a fair bit of blame for the defeat because we never played to our true ability that night at all. We were disgusted by our performance in the match. The anti-climax was compounded when we got to the airport at around nine o'clock the following morning. The Italian authorities kept all the Celtic supporters and us behind and got all the Dutch supporters and the Feyenoord team away first. They stuck the Celtic squad and officials in a room about the same size as someone's front room and we couldn't get sandwiches or tea or anything like that. That was a nightmare; having just been beaten in a European Cup final, the last thing you want to do is sit around an airport all day but we had no option. We didn't take off until about five o'clock in the evening.

It hadn't been a bad achievement for me, as a full-back, to score two goals in two separate European Cup finals but the shine was taken off that by our failure to win the 1970 final. Everybody remembers the winners but nobody remembers the runners-up. I actually tossed my runners-up medal away. On the Saturday evening after the match a few pals were over at our house to have a couple of drinks and I tossed the medal out of the window into the garden. I had no intention of retrieving it, I didn't want it back, but my wife Anne went out and picked it up. I was on a downer after losing the final. I had wanted to have the same feeling in 1970 as I had had in 1967; I had seen the looks on the faces of the Inter players after we had beaten them and now I and my team-mates felt as bad as the Inter guys had done.

Within days of our defeat by Feyenoord, we flew out to North America for a post-season tour. Bertie Auld and I returned earlier than expected when we were sent home from New York. We had been in Kearney, New Jersey, at the behest of one of our supporters' clubs after a match and they took us to a restaurant where there was a graduation and presentation taking place that we were expected to watch. Now we had just played a game and were knackered. All we wanted to do was have a couple of beers and do a bit of sniffing after birds, if there were any around. Instead, we found ourselves hauled into this graduation for about 50 guys and gals, all wearing mortar boards and gowns. Each one made a long-drawn-out speech about how pleased they were to be there that day and how they would like to thank their momma and their poppa, which was all very well but of absolutely no interest to us. Can you imagine sitting listening to that schmaltz for hours? So after we had been there for two hours, I said to Bertie, 'I can't take any more of this. Let's get out of here.' So we went upstairs to the bar and began scooping up the drinks because we didn't have another game for several days. Some of the local supporters' club officials, who ran this club in Kearney, took offence at Bertie and me leaving the presentation so they kicked up a stink with Sean Fallon. Big Jock had left the tour party and gone home, he said, to see wee Jinky, who had been excused from the tour because of his fear of flying, and to discuss a new contract with him. It was only later that we found out that on his return Jock had had an interview for the Manchester United job.

These club officials in Kearney went overboard in describing to Sean what we were alleged to have done and really exaggerated the details. They said we had insulted and ill-treated waitresses, touching them up when they were serving food, but Bertie and I can recall only waiters serving food at that function and no waitresses at all. The officials also said that we had been pissed but we never got pissed until we had left the graduation and gone upstairs to the bar to have a few drinks. Sean phoned big Jock because the supporters' club guys had complained to the tour organisers. Big Jock told Sean simply to pack us off back home on the next available flight.

We had to make our own way to the airport and landed at Prestwick, where we managed to shake off some press guys who had been awaiting us, and went straight to Celtic Park. We told Jock exactly what had happened: we had had a good few drinks; we had never touched up any females because there were no females serving food at the function; we hadn't insulted anybody; and we had just walked out because the graduation ceremony had been so tedious. We had had too much to drink, we never did deny that, but nothing untoward had happened. Jock gave us 100 lines and told us not to do it again but there were no fines or suspensions. The story ran and ran because a reporter, John Mackenzie of the *Scottish Daily Express*, made a song and dance and got headlines out of it for about three days but there was nothing to it. Jock simply said, 'Learn from it and don't let it happen again. It's now over and done with and you've been punished enough through being sent home.' As soon as he saw us face to face, that was the end of the matter. I didn't think we should have been sent home at all because everybody got pissed on that tour at one time or another. We all liked a good drink after a game. If Jock had still been with us out in the States, he would have known how to handle it without it mushrooming into a big scandal.

We thought all the press guys were the same – that you could trust them not to write something if you said it off the record – but this guy Mackenzie was a real ratbag of a pressman. If you told him something off the record, the following day there would be headlines on the front or back page. He was one guy you really couldn't trust because he would stab you in the back as soon as look at you. We had stopped speaking to him but he had obviously heard whispers about our conduct, probably exaggerated by the Kearney guys, and he turned it into a front-page story that featured all sorts of innuendos.

Now and then I did think of withdrawing my transfer request because things continued to go well for the club. We won the Scottish Cup and League Double in the 1970–71 season although Aberdeen gave us a serious challenge for the title, leading the League for a large chunk of that season. We were three points behind them when we met them at Pittodrie in late April 1971 but we drew 1–1 up there and won our two games in hand to take the title for the sixth successive time. On trips to Aberdeen, we used to leave Glasgow on the ten o'clock train and it took three and a half hours to get there, so, when we got into Aberdeen station at half past one, Jock made us walk to Pittodrie, a few miles away, to loosen our legs. All the punters on the train would walk up to Pittodrie with us, talking away. It was different on the way home: the train to Glasgow was at quarter past five so we raced in and out of the showers and had a police escort to the station. On the train we would go straight into relaxation mode and Denis Law's brother, who was a steward on that train, would bring us a supply of vodka and Coke every fifteen minutes. We pulled the shades down so that anyone moving along the corridor would not see us drinking. That was the only time we had a wee chance to relax and unwind like that on our return from a league match because it was the only particularly long trip that we made inside Scotland.

We reached the European Cup quarter-finals that year, losing to Ajax on a 3–1 aggregate in the spring of 1971. Although I retained a regular place in the team and played many more matches than I missed, I did miss a few. I didn't know why. Then, in the 1971–72 season, Jock started leaving me out quite frequently and playing the likes of Jim Brogan or Jimmy Quinn. I'm not really blowing my own trumpet in saying that I was a much better player than both of them. Jock had already disposed of a lot of first-team regulars between 1967 and 1970 and maybe it was his idea to start gradually rebuilding. I could understand that but I couldn't understand why I might be regarded as past it: I was only 27 and had shown that I could still do it at European Cup level. Jock Stein would never offer any explanation as to why he was leaving me out: he would simply say on a Thursday, 'You'll be with the reserves this weekend.'

Very good young players were coming through at Celtic in the early 70s but I never regarded them as a threat because none of them played in my position. David Hay and Danny McGrain filled in at left-back now and then but they were not what you might call natural left-backs; they were better deployed elsewhere on the park. On one occasion at Seamill, Jock brought down some of the most promising young boys for one of his three-day breaks – George Connelly, Davie Hay, Vic Davidson, Kenny Dalglish and Lou Macari – and told us not to lead them astray. So when we were relaxing in the bar, we showed a good example by ordering nothing more than half-pints for ourselves. We asked the boys what they would like to drink and they said they would be happy with Cokes. After a while we looked over and thought they were looking a bit merry, sitting there giggling. We discovered that George Connelly had a bottle of vodka under the table and was emptying it into their Cokes.

Kenny Dalglish was a very promising young footballer but at that stage he played on the right side of midfield. Jock used to blood all the young boys in matches that, on paper, looked easy fixtures and it wasn't until Kenny Dalglish scored six goals out of Celtic's seven in Frank Beattie's testimonial match at Kilmarnock in 1971 that his ability as a goal scorer became apparent to all of us. I was supposed to be on standby to play but I was on the golf course at Dullatur with Willie Wallace on the day of the game. Jock phoned the clubhouse, where we were having a couple of pints. Bill Rankin, the clubmaster, came looking for us and we told him to say that we were still out on the course. It was only after that game at Kilmarnock that Jock started to play Kenny up front. There was no looking back after that. If Willie Wallace had gone down for the game, Jock might not have played Kenny up front that day, but Kenny would still have made his breakthrough in style at some point.

Kenny would go on to become a world-class player with Celtic and Liverpool but the most skilful of the young boys at the club at that time was George Connelly. He had superb ball control and passing ability, he was reasonably good in the air and he could tackle. George eventually drifted away from the game, which was a terrible waste of natural ability. He had personal problems and I think he hit the bevvy badly. He was also shy and couldn't mix with the other players. Big Jock told us to get him into the fold but he would never come for a couple of pints after training and if someone had a party on a Saturday evening he would never come along. Davie Hay, George's great pal, started at right-back then moved into midfield and was an excellent player: very strong, a fine athlete, a great tackler, brave, good in the air, a good marker – a good man to have in your side. Lou Macari was sharp in the box, could turn people and sniff out goals. Vic Davidson was great at running at defenders but he tended to keep the ball at his feet too long instead of passing it. Danny McGrain was a magnificent overlapping full-back who did on the right-hand side what I had been doing for some years on the left. They all had good points; all they needed was experience and the only way you can get experience is by playing in the first team. Most of them made the grade and had lengthy, successful careers in the game, both at Celtic and elsewhere.

Celtic had reached seven successive League Cup finals since the arrival of Jock Stein in 1965 and the 1971 match was against

Partick Thistle. The Firhill side were newly promoted to the top division and we had not yet played them in a League fixture when the League Cup final came around in October. I think there were shades of Feyenoord about that match: we underestimated them but we soon found out just how good a side they were when they went 4–0 up in little over half an hour. They had a lot of useful players and they played well that day. I played at centre-back in that match because Billy McNeill was injured and Jock had to shuffle the team around. I had played there before a couple of times and, when we went down, I made two or three runs forward from central defence to try to find a way to retrieve the situation. Jock shouted at me from the sidelines that there was to be no more of that. Thistle won 4–1 and deserved it. That match at Hampden Park on 23 October 1971 was not only one of the most massive surprises in the history of Scottish football, it also turned out to be my final appearance for Celtic in front of the Celtic supporters. I made just one further appearance for the club, eleven days later, in Malta, in the second leg of a European Cup tie with Sliema Wanderers, a match that was a foregone conclusion as we were 5–0 up from the first leg. We cruised through the game to win 2–1 on a dry, dusty pitch in front of a few thousand Maltese fans. It was not, perhaps, the way I would have wished to end my Celtic playing career but it was what Jock Stein wanted and what Jock Stein wanted he usually got.

8. MOVING ON

Thoughts of European Cup finals or playing for Barcelona were fast receding as I trundled north by British Rail from England to Glasgow in the midwinter of 1971. I had travelled down to the City Ground, the home of Nottingham Forest, shortly before Christmas that year to look into an offer from Forest. It would mean leaving Celtic, who were due shortly to play Ujpest Dozsa of Hungary in the European Cup quarter-finals, to join a Forest side that was in severe danger of relegation from England's top division but I had decided the move was necessary, as it had become clear that Jock Stein felt it was time for me to part company with Celtic. By that stage I had grown very wary of his dishonesty and duplicity regarding potential moves during the time I was available for transfer. So when Forest officials handed me my transfer papers to deliver to Celtic, it was very tempting to open the envelope and ensure that the details of the transfer were exactly as I had been told. A player was due five per cent of the transfer fee and Matt Gillies, the Nottingham Forest manager, had told me that the fee was £40,000, so I was curious to know if that was correct: if the fee had actually been £50,000 or £60,000, then I would have been due more money. Once I got home to Kirkintilloch, I steamed open the envelope and discovered that they had told me the truth – the fee was indeed £40,000. It was about the first time I had been on the end of some straight dealing in the two years since I had gone on the transfer list.

Forty thousand pounds was a reasonable fee for my transfer. Defenders always cost less than forwards, and although a British record fee was set the same month at £220,000, when Alan Ball joined Arsenal from Everton, I felt my fee was a respectable reflection of my worth.

I had been on the transfer list for more than two years when Jock Stein told me about Nottingham Forest's offer. It sounded a bit strange to me that after two years on the transfer list a club should suddenly make an offer for me when I had not appeared in Celtic's first team for six weeks. Jock Stein must have decided that I was surplus to requirements and that it was time to ship me out while the club could still get a decent amount of money for me. He probably felt, after losing the European Cup final to Feyenoord and then the League Cup final to Partick Thistle, that it was time to revamp his team and reorganise things at Celtic Park.

I had just come home after training one Wednesday afternoon when Jock phoned and said, 'Nottingham Forest have made an offer for you. Are you interested in speaking to them?' I said, 'Are you accepting the offer?' He said, 'Yes.' So I said I would speak to them. Jock told me to get a flight down to East Midlands Airport as soon as I could. Willie Henderson and Davie White, the ex-Rangers manager, who had a pub-cum-showbar in Chapelhall, had asked me to go along that night to judge a talent contest. So I booked a flight to the Midlands for the following morning. That evening, as I emerged from the function, wee Jim Rodger, a pressman, was waiting for me. He said in his high-pitched, wheedling voice, 'I hear you're going down south, son.' I said, 'Who told you that, Jim?' 'Och,' he said, 'I know a lot of people.' Now big Jock had said he would keep things quiet regarding my transfer until I had spoken to Forest, so I was wondering how Jim Rodger knew when no other press guy did. I told him I was flying south to talk to a club. He said, 'Is it somewhere in the Midlands, son?' and added that he thought he knew where I was going, saying something about Robin Hood. He had the story in his paper the next morning that I was in talks with Forest.

I reached the City Ground, Nottingham, at around six o'clock on the Thursday evening and met the Forest chairman and Matt Gillies, a fellow Scotsman. The first thing I said was, 'Have Celtic accepted your offer?' They said, 'Yes.' So I was one up right away because I knew that both Forest and Celtic wanted the transfer to happen, and I could do a fair bit of haggling with Forest. I finished up doing OK out of it after four hours of talking about the deal they would offer me. That was on the Thursday evening and I agreed to the details of a three-year contract with Forest just after midnight that night, so I became a Forest player in the early hours of Friday, 17 December 1971. They put me into the Trent Bridge Hotel for the night and I went into the ground to meet the players on the Friday morning and did a wee bit of light training with them. I stayed overnight in the hotel again and went on the team coach with them to Sheffield United for their match at Bramall Lane on the Saturday. Attending that match really brought it home to me that I was in England now: three sides of the ground had terracings and stands but on the fourth side was a cricket pitch. It must have been weird to play on such a ground. I then took the train home from Sheffield.

I was sad to leave Celtic but I realised it was not worth staying. Jock Stein had selected me for only three first-team League games that season so it was clear I was no longer in his plans. I did not want to hang around simply to play in reserve football, especially when the people who had come into the team in my place were not, in my opinion, fit to lace my boots. I just wanted to get to a club where I would not be messed about. It was certainly a backward step football-wise because Nottingham Forest were not one of the elite sides in the First Division of the English Football League. On the other hand, it was a huge leap forward financially. Overnight, I trebled my guaranteed weekly pay. At Forest, I received appearance money, League position money and pointage bonus money, and I got another bonus because I was an international footballer. With all those additions to my basic wage, I ended up with around £180 a week, whereas when I left Celtic the basic wage was £60. Playing in the reserves, as I did quite often in my final season at Celtic Park, I had been stuck with that basic wage and no-win bonuses for a large chunk of 1971. So I had trebled my money just by moving, plus I had a signing-on fee of £2,000 coming my way. It was strange to find myself so much better off after switching from one of Europe's top dogs to a club battling against relegation, especially as Forest were far from the richest club in England.

I had been with Celtic for more than ten years, which suggests that a testimonial might have been in order. I had brought up the subject when I went to see Jock in the summer of 1967 to negotiate a new contract, and had asked him what the possibility would be of having a testimonial match if I was at Celtic for more than ten years. His exact words were, 'As long as I am manager of Celtic Football Club, there will be no testimonial matches.' Three years after I left, while Jock Stein was still Celtic manager, Billy McNeill was given a testimonial match. Four years later, who gets a testimonial match? Jock Stein. I think he allowed Billy to have a testimonial because he was preparing the way for himself; he didn't want to be first to accept a testimonial after vowing they would never happen, did he?

It had hit the press that I had signed for Forest even before I got the chance to take my transfer papers to Celtic Park, so when I went into the ground the boys knew I had left the club. I was the sixth member of the European Cup-winning side to leave and there was a tinge of sadness at saying my farewells to Jinky, Bobby Murdoch, Billy McNeill and Bobby Lennox, although we knew we would always bump into each other in the future. Jock Stein wished me all the best and hoped everything would work out for me. He also, more or less, said that the whole episode shouldn't have happened in the first place and it was a pity it had come to the point of my leaving the club. Then he waved his big left paw at me as if to say there was no point in continuing the discussion and I turned and left his office for the last time.

My first appearance for Nottingham Forest was against Arsenal on 27 December 1971, and you couldn't have squeezed another body into the City Ground that day. It was also wee Alan Ball's first game for Arsenal. Perhaps his transfer from Everton, and mine from Celtic, helped to swell the crowd, although the crowds in the day or two after Christmas are always good in England. I was booked for kicking Ball and he for kicking me. We drew 1–1; a fair result since Arsenal were League champions and FA Cup holders. They gave us the runaround for the first fifteen minutes or so but we went on to play well in the remainder of the match. I was involved in the move for our goal. I got the ball at the back, knocked it forward for Ian Storey-Moore and he went past six

Arsenal players and knocked it past Bob Wilson and into the net for a quite magnificent goal. He was a fine player, pacy with wonderful close control, not unlike Bestie in style, only faster and sharper off his mark, and he could go past players with no trouble at all. George Graham equalised for Arsenal in the second half but 1–1 was a useful result against an Arsenal team that featured players such as Ray Kennedy and John Radford and was chasing the championship again that season. We gave as good as we got that day. It was a fine start and added to the good impression I had been given of the team when I had seen them play at Sheffield United the day after I signed. I used those two matches, particularly the one in which I had played, as a yardstick to gauge how good a side I had joined and decided we weren't bad at all. That was true, but the management left something to be desired.

Leaving Celtic Park for the City Ground was like going on holiday to Butlins. The discipline at Forest was virtually non-existent. We had some good players: Peter Cormack, an established Scotland international; Ian Storey-Moore, who had appeared for England; Neil Martin, who had played three times for Scotland; John Robertson; Martin O'Neill; Tommy Jackson, a Northern Ireland international and a beaverish worker in midfield. Martin O'Neill and John Robertson were both in their late teens. John played on the right-hand side of midfield as a playmaker and Martin was used either in central midfield or up front. Martin liked to get the ball at his feet and run at people – he was a powerful, strong-running young guy – but he sometimes overdid the running with the ball and would get caught in possession. He looked much more sturdily built when he was playing than he does now. Martin was a quiet individual but Robbo was pretty outgoing. There were half a dozen Scots at the club; we would all meet up at the Nottingham Knight pub on a Monday evening and have three or four pints and Robbo would join us. He was keen to be one of the boys, whereas Martin was more self-contained, although on the park he was not quiet: he was always screaming to get the ball to his feet. Both of them were just breaking through to the first team when I arrived at Forest. They didn't play in every game but you could see they were highly enthusiastic and constantly improving. Forest's first team may have been struggling but the club had a very good youth set-up and the guy who looked after my boots was Viv Anderson, who joined the club in 1972 and went on to become the first black footballer to represent England at senior level. I used to call him 'Pele' and he loved that. Tony Woodcock was another youngster at the club. You could see the long-term possibilities, with those young players coming through.

The situation at first-team level, however, was similar to the one I had found when reporting for internationals with Scotland. There was hardly any guidance. The tactical knowledge, the training procedures and even the training ground were all sub-standard in comparison to those at Celtic. They had a training ground by the River Trent and even in the middle of summer the ground was heavy. Training started at ten o'clock and some players would walk in at five to ten and, of course, it was impossible for them to get their clothes off, get their kit on and get down to the training ground by ten. Day after day you would see players jogging alongside the Trent, late for training, but never being fined for it. All they would get would be a smack on the wrist. Some players were fit and some were not; some had a shocking attitude, going through the motions in training and mucking about all the time. In training you are supposed to be sharp and preparing for matchday but you would see players making lax, careless passes and not bothering their backside about it. As with the Scottish national team, the cumulative effect was to undermine the purposefulness and professionalism that are necessary if a football team is going to do anything.

They would give us every Wednesday off and then at ten o'clock on Thursday morning we would go in for training and would be on the running track for two and a half hours, with no sign of a ball. We would do long and short sprints and laps of the track and, in between, would be jogging all the time. Then, as soon as we stopped training, our legs just went stiff because we had had no chance to loosen up our muscles between sprints. I went to the coach, Bob McKinlay, a Scotsman and a former Forest centre-half for whom Celtic had played a testimonial in the 60s. I said to him, 'Why do you do that to us on a Thursday morning? It means that by the final twenty minutes of the game every

Saturday, the legs are hanging off of us and we've got nothing left.' He replied, 'We know what you guys get up to on a Wednesday night at the end of your day off.' He was referring to how six or seven of us would go to a local pub and have a few drinks. He added, 'We've got to run it out of your systems on a Thursday morning.' So I said to him, 'Why don't you give us a Monday off and then murder us on a Tuesday so that we have four days for our legs to recover? We would then have plenty left for the last twenty minutes on a Saturday.' He said, 'No, we can't do that. The manager plays golf on a Wednesday.'

I had received a boost from moving club and making a fresh start, but I had been there for several months before I scored a goal. Matt Gillies said, 'Well, that took a while, didn't it?' I think he had been expecting me to score every week.

Forest had been in the lower half of the top division in England when I joined and, although relegation was a threat, it did look easily avoidable. That changed when, in early 1972, we suffered eight successive defeats. Once you get two or three defeats, never mind eight, the heads go down. We went to play Leeds United in late March and with the score at 1–1 in the first half I began charging forward to help start attacks and look for a second goal for us as we needed the points. Gillies and McKinlay told me at half-time, 'You'll need to stay back and defend. You can't charge forward. We need to protect what we have and drawing 1–1 would be a good result for us here at Elland Road.' I had an argument with them over them being happy with a draw and the match ended up with us being beaten 6–1. I could not believe it.

I became a fixture in the Forest side for the rest of that season, scoring six goals. The game that stood out was one against Chelsea, who were going like a bomb at that time, with Dave Sexton as manager, but we beat them and I scored twice. One of the goals was a screamer from about 25 yards with my left peg; Peter Bonetti was in goal for Chelsea. After the game I went into my local pub for two or three pints, as I always did. I didn't need to buy a drink that night. The following week the Cheltenham Festival was taking place, so I went down on the Wednesday with Ian Storey-Moore, Peter Hindley and Peter Cormack, who were very keen on the horses. While I was there I met the Chelsea winger I had played against, and he told me his instructions had been that when I went forward he was to go back with me and shut me out. Then at half-time Sexton had said, 'Don't bother picking up Gemmell if he goes forward.' It was in the second half that I scored both of my goals so their tactic backfired on them.

Football in England was not played any faster than it was in Scotland but it was harder to get the ball off your opponents. There were also a lot more individually skilful players in England, and more teams with useful collective ability. I found no problem in adjusting to the game down there but playing for Forest did not help my Scotland career at all. There was so much talent available to Scotland at the time that there was little question of a player who was with a club in Forest's position – in the relegation zone of the First Division – being brought into the squad for the national team. If I hadn't left Celtic I am sure I would have won more caps.

I stayed in hotels for the first three months of my time at Forest and Anne would come down each weekend, or else I would go home, depending on where we were playing. If we were playing in London, for example, I would just fly home. Then, in March 1972, I bought a house in Burton Joyce, a wee village about five miles east of Nottingham; Neil Martin lived about 50 yards away, Peter Cormack lived 100 yards down the hill and next door to Neil lived Jimmy Sirrell, who had played for Celtic and was the manager of Notts County. I wanted to be close to guys I knew, such as Neil and Peter; I had played against them both when they had been at Hibs. It was a busy time: my son David was conceived in Nottingham and after Anne and Karen Michelle had moved into our new house, David was born there, in 1972. I sold my house in Kirkintilloch to my mother-in-law.

Matt Gillies was a quiet, well-spoken guy, although he tended to ramble on and be unspecific when it came to his team talks. He would say something like, 'Now this is a right good side we're playing today, boys, we'll have to be at our best to get a result. I want you to keep everything shipshape and bristol fashion.' We would be none the wiser than we had been before he started speaking. He was a nice man but that doesn't win you games. I don't think I ever saw him lose his temper. McKinlay used to do all the shouting for him. They would talk about things in the dugout while the game was going on, then McKinlay would come in at half-time and lay into whoever was to get a lecture and Matt Gillies would just stand in the background. I wasn't too keen on McKinlay: you sometimes had the impression that he thought he was just that wee step above you, a wee bit superior. The coach is supposed to be the buffer between the manager and the players, and to get on well with the players, but McKinlay behaved like a sergeant-major towards us at all times.

We had a training session one day when McKinlay picked a team of eleven players and we lined up in one half without anybody in the other half: we were playing against nobody. He wanted us to build up the game and play as if we were in a match situation, but how do you do that if there is no opposition? All we were doing was knocking passes to each other, with nobody intercepting them. So we knocked it back and forth all the way up the field until it reached Neil Martin and he knocked it into the net, past the ghost goalkeeper. I burst out laughing. Afterwards we asked each other what that exercise had achieved.

The lack of discipline at Forest caused us to plummet down the table and face the prospect of relegation at the end of the 1971–72 season. That was compounded by the club deciding to sell its better players. Ian Storey-Moore, the man with the pace in our attack, was sold to Manchester United in March 1972 for £200,000 and later that year Peter Cormack left for Liverpool for a fee of £110,000. That deprived us of our two major creators and scorers of goals. They were never replaced. If you lose quality attacking players and do not replace them, something's got to give. We were also far from watertight at the back. We had a goalkeeper, Jim Barron, who might have a great game or might toss the ball into the back of the net. On his bad days, he was liable to let the ball go through his legs, or to go down trying to stop a shot and end up palming it into the net. On his good days, nothing would get past him. We lacked a bit of pace in the middle of the defence, where Sammy Chapman and Peter Hindley were the two centre-backs. They were both big, strong guys who were good in the air and strong in the tackle but would be outrun by any forward with the slightest bit of sharpness.

Towards the end of that season, our relegation rivals Crystal Palace came to the City Ground and, in one of those ironic moments that are often thrown up by football, Willie Wallace, who had been transferred to Palace a few weeks before I left for Forest, scored the goal that relegated us. Still, in April 1972, when they won their seventh successive League title, Celtic sent me a League winner's medal, which was something I appreciated, especially as I had played in only three Scottish League matches that season.

Relegation didn't affect me financially because in the lower division we would receive more win bonuses, but you still want to stay in the top division. It was an entirely new experience for me to play in relegation battles and go to places such as Oxford or Hull. Football was more physical at that level and it was difficult to grind out games at such venues after having been used to European Cup finals and playing in top-class stadiums on the continent. A lot of my team-mates at Forest lost much of their appetite for the game during that season and it probably affected me, subconsciously, as well. It was a very difficult division to escape from, especially after we had sold our premier players. We had hoped to be down for one season and then bounce straight back up but the matches were a lot harder than we had anticipated, and things were more frantic at that level. Players in the top division would knock the ball about and run off the ball but in the lower division, as soon as you had the ball, players would be snapping at your ankles immediately. They made up for their lack of ability with a higher work-rate.

We struggled to adjust at the lower level and after thirteen League matches we were eighth in the table. We had gone out of the League Cup in our opening tie of the competition, losing 1–0 at home to Aston Villa, and had won only four League matches, all by a single goal. Our four defeats included a 3–0 loss at Queen's Park Rangers and going down 4–1 to Sunderland at Roker Park after opening the season drably with 0–0 draws at home to Portsmouth and away to Hull. It was less than inspiring and there was no suggestion that Matt Gillies could turn it around, so he was removed from his position in mid-October 1972 to be replaced in early November by Dave Mackay, the former Scotland international. I had been ever-present in the team until that point and I even scored in Mackay's first game in charge, a 3–2 victory over Millwall at home that took us into fifth position. Three games later, I was dropped and replaced at left-back by John Winfield. I was out of the team for a month and then returned at right-back for two matches in place of Peter Hindley. The second, a 1–0 defeat at Oxford on 6 January 1973, which saw the club drop down to thirteenth position, was my final match for Forest. I had been at the club for little more than a year.

Dave Mackay and his assistant, Des Anderson, were both from Edinburgh and they had been manager and coach together at Swindon Town prior to joining Forest. There was a bit of dig about Mackay and he wanted to freshen things up in his own way but his efforts were occasionally almost as eccentric as those of the previous management team. He would come down to the training ground and during the training session all he would do would be to play keepy-uppy on his own, have a look around and then go back to doing a bit more keepy-uppy. It was Des Anderson who did all the coaching and told us which exercises to do in training. Dave Mackay was rather aloof and didn't give much away; neither did Des Anderson. Tactically, things improved and Mackay's team talks were better than Gillies' but they badly needed players and there was no money to buy them. The sum the club had received from selling its best players had been needed to meet the wages bill and running costs because they had suffered a shortfall in gate money after relegation: the average crowd at the City Ground when Forest were in the First Division had been close to 22,000 but relegation reduced the average attendance by more than half, to under 10,000. Gate money was by far the major source of income for football clubs in the '70s.

With Mackay's arrival, my position was under threat. I believe he wanted someone in my position who would be more defensively minded and less interested in roving forward, as I had always enjoyed doing. An attacking full-back such as myself was probably a luxury he could not afford if the club was to battle its way back into the First Division. At that point, the same pressman who had tried to help me move to Barcelona and Leicester City gave me a call and asked if I would like to go to Dundee. Forest agreed and we came to an amicable financial settlement to release me from my contract. I also received a nice signing-on fee from Dundee.

I had never had any hankering after a return home because I really enjoyed living in Nottingham. The River Trent flowed through Burton Joyce, so you could go for river walks, and there were two pleasant local pubs. I was never restless or homesick, never wanted to leave; I was settled in the Midlands in our friendly village with good neighbours and enjoyed the company of my team-mates at Forest. But once a manager decides you are out of the picture there is little point in remaining at a club.

One beautiful Friday night towards the end of that 1972–73 season I decided to go out with my Flymo and cut my grass – I wasn't playing the following day. The Flymo took a bit of a jump against a stone and the machine sliced off the top of my right toe at a 45-degree angle. I tied a tourniquet round it to stop the bleeding, my missus phoned Neil Martin and he came and took me to the general hospital in Nottingham. The surgeon who worked on the toe in Accident & Emergency performed a magnificent operation. He sat me up on the table and gave me a local anaesthetic and I watched him cut bits off my toe and pull out the toenail, take a skin-graft off my left arm, place it over my toe and stitch it on. He restored my toe so well that it looked exactly as it had done before the accident. Neil took me back home and on the way we stopped at an off-licence and I got a bottle of vodka, not for fun but because I needed it. Once the local anaesthetic wore off I was in agony and the vodka helped to kill the pain. I couldn't kick a ball for about three months after that because the blade of the lawnmower had damaged the nerve and any pressure on the toe put me in agony. I could walk about but I had to wear a sandshoe with the toe cut away. Eventually the nerve healed and everything returned to normal and I never had any problems with it after that.

I had few regrets about leaving Forest because lower league football was not to my taste at all. I had become rather disillusioned by the type of football I was facing, and it was obvious that Forest weren't going anywhere fast; they finished fourteenth in the Second Division that season and made a quick exit from the FA Cup. There seemed to be a lack of ambition among the key people at the club and that helped me to decide it was time to leave. Dave Mackay stayed only a few months longer, and then, after Allan Brown had been manager for little more than a year, Brian Clough would arrive at the City Ground in January 1975. He transformed Forest by shaking up everyone at the club and then in successive seasons won them promotion, led them to the League title and, amazingly, guided them on to win the European Cup in 1979. The left-back in Forest's European Cup-winning side in Munich in 1979 was Frank Clark, who was 35, exactly the same age as I was that year. If I had held on at Forest and seen out my contract for its two remaining years, Cloughie might have got the best out of me. A second European Cup winner's medal would have been a very nice way of rounding off my playing career.

9. TAY DAYS

An ambitious attitude at Dundee had drawn me to that club and that ambition was rewarded in style mere months after my arrival at Dens Park. The first major trophy up for grabs on my return to Scotland was the League Cup and, with me as captain, Dundee streaked to the final and lifted the trophy on a memorable day at Hampden Park in December 1973. The occasion was laden with poignancy for me: our opponents were Celtic and Dundee even relied on the intervention of an old foe of mine to clinch the Cup. We had gone 1–0 ahead with fifteen minutes remaining, when Gordon Wallace, our striker, eluded the challenges of a posse of Celtic defenders, turned on the ball just inside the penalty area and shot past Ally Hunter in the Celtic goal. We were still ahead in the final minute when Celtic's Jimmy Johnstone collected the ball in the centre circle and began one of those mazy runs of his. He went past several of our defenders and was one on one with Thomson Allan, our goalkeeper, when the referee, Bobby Davidson, blew his whistle to end the match. Jimmy had been seconds away from putting the ball in the net. Davidson hated Celtic and he had always acted against the club in the matches he refereed. He took charge of eight Old Firm matches, of which Celtic won not one, and, most notably, he had swayed the 1970 Scottish Cup final Aberdeen's way with a display of refereeing that was clearly biased against Celtic. Now his hatred of Celtic had worked in my favour.

That League Cup final should never actually have gone ahead. The park was almost waterlogged; if you made a pass, you could see jets of spray springing up as the ball flew across the turf. Scotland had been under snow prior to the Saturday of the match but there had been a thaw on the morning of the game, leaving the pitch like a swamp. Davidson still decided to play the match. Other unusual circumstances surrounded that final. It took place at the time of an energy crisis in Britain and the government had declared a state of emergency that forbade the use of floodlights at football grounds. So the game kicked off at 1.30 p.m. and we made a three-hour coach journey down to Hampden from Dundee on the morning of the match, with only a 25-minute break for a very early lunch.

My own preparation for the match had been less than ideal. On the previous evening I had come down to Glasgow by train to carry out an interview for the Scottish Television show *Scotsport* with Alex Cameron. It was 'live' and the programme was not being broadcast until late in the evening. I did the interview just after ten o'clock and the television people then sped me down to Queen Street station to catch the last train to Dundee. There was snow on the ground everywhere and the train had no heating so I was freezing cold for several hours. By the time I got home and into my bed it was about one o'clock in the morning. It had still been a worthwhile journey because on the programme I had made it clear, as Dundee captain, that we were not going to go as lambs to the slaughter: we had good goal scorers, a strong defence and imaginative midfielders, just like Celtic. All of our players who were watching the programme would, I imagine, have been given a boost on hearing that.

We played well at Hampden Park that day; it wasn't as if we stole it. Celtic were at full strength, with players such as Danny McGrain, Davie Hay, George Connelly and Kenny Dalglish, and Jimmy Johnstone had been given a roving role by big Jock. It was an evenly balanced match and, although both sides had chances, it turned out to be our day. The good Scottish clubs outside of the Old Firm were able to compete closely with Celtic and Rangers during the early '70s: if we played Celtic ten times we would expect to win four or five times. There were a lot of good players in Scotland, almost all Scots, and it wasn't possible for them all to be concentrated at the two biggest clubs.

The climax to any cup final is raising the trophy above your head but when Dundee won the League Cup in 1973 I was quite embarrassed, as captain, when I was going up the steps at Hampden to lift the trophy. All of Jock Stein's cronies, those businessmen who had accompanied us on trips abroad with Celtic so often and whose faces were so well known to me, had secured the best seats at Hampden through big Jock, and I had to go past them to lift the trophy that I had helped to deny Celtic. If we had beaten Rangers, I would have been doing handstands, but after beating Celtic I could understand how those Celtic supporters felt: only two years previously I had been on the losing Celtic side in a League Cup final against Partick Thistle. I found it an awkward situation but the business people turned out to be brilliant about it, saying we had deserved the win and should enjoy our night of celebration. I held the Cup up and then passed it on to Thomson Allan, behind me, as quickly as I could. It was quite an embarrassing moment but overall I was delighted for Dundee, the Dundee supporters and myself.

I had never anticipated such swift success at my new club. It was the first thing Dundee had won since the great days of such players as Alan Gilzean, Andy Penman and Alex Hamilton, who had all been part of the side that had won the League title in 1962. Davie White, the former Rangers manager, was in charge of Dundee when I returned to Scottish football and he had been a good manager of Rangers in the late 60s; they had pushed Celtic all the way in the 1967–68 season and had almost snatched that title, our third in a row, from us. They lost just one game all season and ended up only two points behind us after suffering their only defeat in their final match. Davie White had a good knowledge of football and was a good talker on the game, although he maybe talked too much. His right-hand man was big Harry Davis, who had played with Rangers in the early '60s. He was the trainer and coach at Dundee and the hard man of the partnership. Davie tended to stay in the background and let Harry do all the rough stuff.

Davie White had made me captain immediately on my arrival at the club and I saw it as my task to give the players a good shake up because it was obvious to me that quite a few of them had been going through the motions. They were going out and playing well but they were not trying hard enough. We soon became a hard side to beat. Dundee had a good squad and, although there were no magnificent players, they had a lot of skilled professionals and they worked very well as a team. Gordon Wallace had been Scottish Footballer of the Year in 1968 and his fellow forward Jocky Scott possessed a lot of trickery and was a very slick type of player. Harry Davis murdered us at training so that made us a very fit side. As at Forest, we had one day on the track when we were given a really hard time but, unlike at Forest, it was done on a Tuesday so our legs had plenty of time to recover before the match on Saturday. I gave my full commitment to every game in which I played for the dark blues. It was during my time at Dens Park that I was sent off for only the second time in my career, playing for Dundee against Motherwell in a League match. My offence was swearing, for which I was fined £5.

Early in 1974, I appeared at Celtic Park for the first time in a Dundee shirt and, as captain, it was my duty to lead the team out. I made a point of taking the players out before Celtic had left their dressing room and I led the team to the 'Celtic end' of the stadium; traditionally the away team would go to the other end of the field, where the away support would be gathered, but I was determined to do it differently. I got a tremendous ovation from the Celtic fans but after the game big Jock said to me, 'You had a cheek on you, taking your team to the Celtic end.' I said, 'You've got to get every advantage you can get in this game, boss, haven't you?' It wouldn't have helped his mood that we had won 2–1.

We did pretty well in my first season at Dundee, winning the League Cup, finishing fifth in the League and qualifying for the UEFA Cup in the subsequent, 1974–75, season. We were drawn against Twente Enschede of Holland in the opening round of that competition and lost both legs of the tie: 3–1 at Dens Park and 4–2 in Enschede. They had two players whom they used through the middle of their attack who looked as though they were in preparation for the Olympic 100 metres. Iain Phillip and George Stewart, our centre-backs, were useful players but they were not blessed with a lot of pace and these Dutch guys absolutely destroyed them. Twente played a holding game inside their own half and then hit us on the break and those two attacking players, with their pace, could not be caught. Twente were a top-class outfit, and the following season would see them reach the final of the UEFA Cup. Dundee were a good side but we were a bit below the standard of the better European clubs and, during the 70s, club football in Belgium and Holland was as strong as it has ever been. That was emphasised the following season. We had finished sixth in the League at the end of the 1974–75 season and had qualified again for the UEFA Cup but once again we were given a tough draw in the opening round, one that sent us back to the Low Countries. This time we faced RWD Molenbeek of Belgium and we lost 4–2 in Dundee and 1–0 in Brussels. Molenbeek were eliminated in the following round of the UEFA Cup by none other than Twente Enschede, as the Dutch side made their way to that year's final.

Those were good matches to play in, as were the Dundee derbies. There would be a full house for those games, whether the match was at Tannadice or Dens Park. The atmosphere was always good and there were always more supporters for Dundee than for Dundee United; Dundee have always been the better supported of the two clubs in the city. Even if Dundee were away in the derby, they would have more support because there were no restrictions on to whom tickets would be sold. So two-thirds of the crowd at every derby would be behind Dundee. It was a mini-version of Celtic v. Rangers but to me it was a dawdle. At Celtic, in the days leading to a Rangers game, you had to get yourself psyched up, but Dundee v. Dundee United, to me, was no more nerve-wracking than a normal game. It was different for the punters in Dundee: to them it was life or death. Some of the Dundee players would comment that I didn't seem too bothered in advance of a Dundee derby. I'd say, 'Are you kidding me? Compared to Celtic v. Rangers, this is like playing in a reserve match.' The Dundee-based players could not believe my nonchalance; to them, the Dundee derby was the height of intensity but, of course, they had never been involved in a Celtic v. Rangers match.

The effect of the Dundee derby on the town was quite noticeable. Graham Thomson, one of the Dundee directors, was managing director of Timex, the town's biggest employer, and he said that, on any Monday morning after Dundee had been beaten, the absenteeism at the factory was horrendous – especially if the defeat had been suffered in a local derby. Is it worth losing a day's wages because your team has been defeated in a game of football? I couldn't fathom it. Surely you should still go to work and get your pay. If you get stick one Monday then all you do is wait until your workmates' team next gets beaten and hand out some stick yourself. The Dundee supporters could not face their Dundee United-supporting workmates on the Monday morning and it was mainly Dundee supporters that worked at the Timex factory. There was a bias, let's say, towards employing the type of people who supported Dundee. There was not supposed to be any religious divide in Dundee but it was there: Dundee were supposedly the Protestants' team and United the Catholics'.

Since joining Dundee in 1973 I had found that pre-season training was becoming harder and harder for me, and that helped me to decide to put the wheels in motion for the day I would have to retire from playing. During my initial year at Dundee I had lived in a stone villa in the town but in the summer of 1974 I had moved out to the small town of Errol, halfway between Dundee and Perth, after purchasing Errol's Commercial Hotel, a nineteenth-century building, for £34,000. It was a good, thriving business, with a number of regular customers and, although it was nominally a hotel, I never let out more than two of the six rooms; that was the minimum necessary to maintain a hotel licence and if you had a hotel licence, your premises enjoyed more liberal licensing laws than public houses. During my twenties, I had barely cast a thought towards the future. I had been too busy living it up and enjoying the perks of being a young footballer. On entering my thirties, it hit home that my days as a player were numbered, so I had purchased the Commercial Hotel as a nest egg for the future.

The ten-team Premier Division that spearheaded the most radical restructuring Scottish football has ever seen was introduc-ed for the 1975–76 season and it proved ominous for Dundee. Prior to the invention of the Premier Division, a club such as Dundee, with one of the bigger supports in Scotland, could be almost certain they were not going to be relegated from an eighteen-team division so they could afford to play a bit expansively. The Premier Division, which was limited to the top ten clubs in the country, each playing the others four times, made relegation much likelier and Scottish football at the top level became much more cut-throat. Dundee had not known relegation since the 1930s but in that 1975–76 season it suddenly loomed ominously on the horizon. St Johnstone were relegated long before the end of that initial Premier Division season – they finished on only eleven points – and Dundee, Dundee United and Aberdeen all finished immediately above them on the same number of points – 32. Dundee had the worst goal difference of the three so it was we who were relegated.

For Dundee's first season in the new second tier of Scottish football, the First Division, I moved to centre-back. I had previously been left-back but in 1976, following our demotion, George Stewart, one of our centre-backs, was transferred to Hibs and Iain Phillip to Crystal Palace. They had been our two central defenders when we had won the League Cup in 1973 but the club's relegation meant that money was needed and the transfer of Phillip, in particular, brought in the cash. I had played several times in the middle of the defence for Celtic, on occasions on which Billy McNeill had been injured; also, I had maybe lost a yard in pace by that time – I was 32 at the beginning of the 1976–77 season – so moving inside to centre-back prevented me being exposed to fast-moving wingers. Davie Johnston slipped into the left-back position and I felt quite comfortable at centre-back. We did moderately well in our first season in the First Division, finishing third, eleven points behind St Mirren and seven behind Clydebank, both of whom were promoted to the Premier Division.

I went on holiday to Majorca at the end of that 1976–77 season and when I returned to Scotland I discovered that Davie White had paid the price for our failure to win promotion at the first attempt: he had been given the sack. Ian Gellatly, the chairman of Dundee, asked me if I could recommend anyone for the manager's job and I suggested wee Bertie Auld, who was doing very well as manager of Partick Thistle. I phoned Bertie and asked if he fancied a stint at Dundee. He said he would talk to them so beforehand he came up to the Commercial Hotel, where I gave him all the details about the directors and what to expect from them. He went to Dens Park for the interview but I think he was really using Dundee's interest in him as a lever to get more dough out of Miller Reid, the Thistle chairman. I don't think Bertie really wanted to go to Dundee because he had his roots in the west of Scotland, had had a house near Larkhall for years and didn't want to uproot himself. Bertie actually ended his interview by saying, 'You've got a manager on your own doorstep.' The directors said, 'Who's that?' Bertie said, 'It's Tommy Gemmell.' So Bertie won himself improved conditions at Thistle and secured for me an interview for the Dundee manager's job.

The directors asked me what I would do if I got the job. I told them the first thing I would do would be to have a clearout. They asked me who I would dispose of but I told them that that was something I would be willing to reveal only if I was given the job. A lot of faces on the playing staff had changed since 1973, when I had first joined the club, and there were a few bad apples in the dressing room. Several guys were always moaning about one thing or another, whether it was money or training gear or tactics, and I was determined to remove them as soon as I became manager.

I asked the directors if they had any money. No, they said, and there was no possibility of getting any. That did make me think twice about taking the job: with no money to spend on the playing staff it was going to be a stern task to lift the club out of the First Division and into the Premier Division. I had to weigh up the knowledge that I could continue as a player for another couple of years with the possibility that I might never again be offered the chance to become manager of a football club. Although Dundee might have been short of money, it was a club of some stature, one that had won the League title and cups and competed in Europe. There was no reason why similar successes might not be achieved in the future. I went back to the board after a couple of days and told them that I had decided to take the job. I then named half a dozen players whom I wished to show the door. There were a couple of funny looks in relation to one or two of the names, as if to suggest that it was not a good idea to get rid of them, but, of course, none of the directors raised any objections. They didn't know those players the way I knew them: they might have thought those players were pulling their weight, but I knew they were not, and there was no point in the board offering me the job if they were not going to allow me to shape the playing squad as I wished.

Once the directors had given me the job of manager they asked if I wanted to continue playing. I wasn't quite ready to stop, and felt fit enough to carry on playing for another couple of seasons, so I again took a few days to think things over. I decided that I could not combine management with playing if I was to do full justice to my new job. If you are player–manager and you need to lay into a player at half-time, it is very difficult to do that unless you are having a very good game in your own right. If you are having a stinker yourself, who gives *you* a hard time at half-time?

One of my first actions as manager, almost as soon as I took over, was to transfer Bobby Hutchinson, a forward, by swopping him for Eric Schaedler, the impressive Hibs left-back. That immediately strengthened our defence. During the three years in which I managed Dundee, there were to be 38 face changes at the club; the whole place had to be freshened up. Gordon Strachan was a 20-year-old midfielder on the playing staff when I became manager but I had to pick and choose his games in the First Division because opponents would kick lumps out of him. They knew that he could play a wee bit so I had to play him against reasonable footballing sides, against whom he could come into his own. If you played him against sides who had hatchet men in the middle of the park he would get done in by the first or second tackle.

My greatest coup as a manager was to clinch the signing of Jimmy Johnstone at the beginning of my first season. I phoned him in the summer of 1977 – he had left Celtic two years previously and had become a free agent after a spell with Sheffield United – and asked him how he fancied coming up to Dundee. He was still only 32 but I told him that if I was to sort out a contract for him it would have to be related to his appearances and his performances. We offered him a two-year deal with a moderate basic wage but a very good signing-on fee spread over the length of the contract and the incentive of excellent bonuses related to appearances. He would also, whenever he played, receive bonuses for points gained and the club's position in the

League. If he played in every one of our games he would earn 50 per cent more than I was receiving myself as manager. I was on £10,000 a year, which was comparable with the income of Jock Stein, whose basic salary, before bonuses, was also £10,000 (he earned £12,100 in that 1977–78 season), or of Ally MacLeod, the new Scotland manager, who was on £15,000 per annum.

Jimmy was very interested in my offer but the only sticking point was the amount of travelling he would have to do between his home in Lanarkshire and Dundee. I told him he could avoid that by staying with me in my hotel in Errol and going home at the weekend to see Agnes, his wife, and their children. That swayed him to agree to the deal but I gave him a strong reminder, as he signed, that he had to play to make the deal fully worthwhile for him. There was no point in signing him if he was only going to sit in the stand: that was why the deal was so firmly linked to appearance money. The directors were delighted at Jimmy's arrival at the club: with him in the team they were guaranteed to recoup the additional payments to him through the revenue generated by several thousand extra people coming through the turnstiles.

Once Jimmy's signing was revealed to the press, Dundee went into uproar. The local papers and the national press went huge on the whole thing and there was real excitement in the town at the prospect of the great Jimmy Johnstone joining Tommy Gemmell and Willie Wallace, whom I had appointed as one of my coaches. The phone never stopped ringing with press guys wanting to speak to wee Jimmy and we received magnificent publicity just from having him at the club. On match days, every time the ball went to his feet a hush descended on the terraces and stands. You could hear a pin drop as the crowd waited for things to happen and when he was on song he could go past players and create goal-scoring opportunities just as he had done in his heyday. The crowd would go into hysterics, willing him on to do his magic.

The only problem was that Jimmy had lost some of his fitness so we had to battle to get him fit. He would work hard enough in training – he was always a tremendous trainer – but then he started mucking about in the afternoons. I would not get back to my hotel from the ground until almost five in the afternoon because of my responsibilities as manager, and wee Jimmy soon grew tired of going back to Errol on his own because there was not much there for him to do except go for a walk or do a bit of fishing in the Tay. So he would remain in Dundee during the afternoons and go out with two or three of the players after training and have an afternoon drinking session with them and all the pals he had got to meet in Dundee. I had deliberately not given him a set of keys for the hotel. That way, I would know what time he came back from the town because he would have to rap the door or ring the bell to gain entry. Soon enough, he began to come back at one o'clock or half past one in the morning and I would be taking him to training in the morning, telling him to screw the nut because the more he drank and the more he lost fitness, the less likely it was that I would play him. I reminded him how much money he was losing by not playing.

One morning he rattled the door at half past three. I let him in, but this was pushing me to the limit. I took him into training later that morning and he was still half-drunk and smelling like a brewery. Dundee trained in the grounds of Strathmartin Hospital, where there was a playing field with a beautiful, lush surface, at the foot of a big hill. So I said to Wispy Wallace, 'Give that wee man a doing this morning. Get him to run from the bottom to the top of that hill and back down twelve times, carrying a medicine ball, and have a different player race up the hill alongside him as his pacemaker every time.' Jimmy did it but you could see he was cursing us under his breath. He was violently sick after the third run but he continued and completed the task. Once he was finished there, we gave him another exercise for stamina; again with the medicine ball. He was to begin at the corner flag, run to the eighteen-yard line and back to the corner flag; then to the halfway line and back to the corner flag; then to the eighteen-yard line at the other end of the field and back to the corner flag; then to the opposite corner flag and back. He had to do that eight times. He saw it through and never said a word. I said to him, 'We've got to get you fit to get you this money. I'm desperate to give you all this money.'

After three months, Willie and I could see we were hitting our heads against a brick wall with Jimmy. We couldn't get him fit; no matter how much punishment we doled out to him at training we couldn't prevent him over-indulging in the drink during his free time. I said to Wispy, 'This is not going to work.' We got Jimmy in one autumn morning and I said to him, 'Wee man, this isn't working.' He said, 'Aye, I know, I'm missing Agnes and the weans.' I burst out laughing. I said, 'What! It's the first time in your life you've missed Agnes and the weans.' I couldn't believe he was saying that. Wispy burst out laughing as well.

I produced a sheet of paper that I had asked the club secretary to prepare in advance of our meeting. It was a waiver that we had had typed up for Jimmy to sign, stating that his contract with Dundee Football Club was cancelled with immediate effect. Jimmy could have held us to ransom because he had had only one instalment of his signing fee and he had a two-year deal with Dundee under which we would have had to pay him his basic wage. I told him that if he signed the waiver I would give him the second part of his signing fee immediately and he signed the form right away. It was a shame because he still had the ability to light up a game and it would have done us all a power of good if he had made the most of that opportunity. Attendances had risen through people being drawn to Dens Park to see Jimmy play, which had kept the directors happy, and he had the ability to lift the team every time he played. It had been Jimmy's last opportunity to revive his talent with a League club and it was a pity it fell through because he still had a lot to offer if he had applied himself fully. Sometimes these things work out; sometimes they don't.

One Monday morning in November 1977, Ian Gellatly, the chairman, said to me, 'We need £50,000 by Friday.' The bank had told him that unless they received that sum of money from Dundee Football Club, they would close the doors of Dens Park. Billy McNeill, who was manager of Aberdeen, had been doing a wee bit of sniffing after Gordon Strachan, but I had told him Strachan was not available because I knew that, if we won promotion to the Premier Division, he would be able to shine at that level. So I phoned Billy up, told him the situation at Dundee, said I would sell Strachan to raise the necessary funds, but made it clear that he would not be getting him for £50,000; he would need to come up with a lot more than that to purchase the player.

After some negotiations, we received £85,000 plus Jim Shirra. The money went straight into the bank and Dundee survived to fight another day.

I would go to Jock Stein on occasion to try to obtain players for Dundee but dealing with him proved to be frustrating. One player I wanted desperately was Brian McLaughlin, who had been a hugely promising midfield player at Celtic in the early 70s but had suffered a severe knee injury at the age of eighteen, which had set back his progress and more or less confined him to reserve-team football. He was not as fit or as sharp as he had been but he was a great passer of the ball and still only 22 years old when, in late 1977, I phoned big Jock to ask about the prospect of signing him. I knew Brian might be available for me to sign because one of the Celtic players had told me that there had been talk around the club that Brian McLaughlin might be getting a free transfer. I asked big Jock, 'Is Brian McLaughlin available?' He replied, 'Oh, I don't know about that.' 'Well, he's not playing in your first-team, is he?' 'Oh, that's true,' Jock responded, 'but I don't know about letting him go. If he is available, though, we would need money for him.' That meant he *was* available. So I said, 'What sort of money are you talking about?' Jock said, in that calculatedly vague way of his, 'Oh, I don't know. Can you come back with an offer?'

I required a ball player in the middle of the park to complement the workers and runners that I had at Dundee and McLaughlin fitted the bill perfectly. So I went to the chairman, told him the story and said that big Jock was looking for money. I asked the directors if there were enough funds available for me to offer £10,000 for the player. The chairman agreed that I could make such an offer; if Celtic asked for a higher transfer fee, Dundee would go as high as £15,000. I immediately phoned big Jock and told him that although we were close to skint, Dundee could offer £10,000 for McLaughlin. Jock said, 'Leave it with me and phone me back at half past nine in the morning.' The following morning I rang him back. 'Oh,' said Jock, 'we've just done a deal. We've signed Joe Filippi from Ayr United for £15,000 and we've given Brian McLaughlin to Ayr as part of the deal.' That was a terrible deal for Celtic: Joe Filippi lasted for only two undistinguished years, while the following season Brian McLaughlin was named

First Division player of the year at Ayr before moving on to Motherwell.

Jock had known that Brian McLaughlin would be a good player for me, and at the time Dundee were looking good for promotion from the First Division to the Premier Division, so I believe he was concerned that if Brian joined Dundee he might eventually do some damage to Celtic. Ayr, in contrast, were heading for relegation from the Premier Division. That would be one reason why he didn't want to sell Brian McLaughlin to me; the other would be that he didn't want to do me a favour. Bertie Auld, when manager of Partick Thistle, and Billy McNeill, as manager of Aberdeen, also approached Jock for players and both found invisible barriers. Billy had tapped Bobby Lennox for a move to Aberdeen and Bobby was very keen to go but even though Bobby was not getting a game for the first team at Celtic by the 1977–78 season, Jock refused to contemplate allowing him to move to Pittodrie. Bertie Auld found Jock similarly difficult to deal with, but Bertie matched big Jock for wiliness. Jock was desperate to sign Ronnie Glavin, the Partick Thistle midfielder, when Bertie was manager at Firhill. Bertie kept stalling him and telling him he wasn't selling the player to Jock. He reminded Jock of the players he had refused to sell to Bertie and told Jock there were top English clubs keen to sign Glavin, which was rubbish. Glavin had been tapped heavily by big Jock and was agitating for a move from Thistle. Eventually Bertie pushed the fee for Glavin to the height of what he knew Celtic could afford – £80,000 – and, with big Jock forced into a corner, Celtic paid up.

Jock did not want anyone who had been a player in any of his teams to go on to be successful elsewhere either as a player or as a manager of other clubs. He was obstructive towards his former players in their transfer dealings and, when it came to transferring players, he always attempted to sell them to clubs of a lower status where the player would find it difficult to thrive – as he did when selling me to Nottingham Forest. I don't know why he took that negative approach, because it would surely have been a compliment to him if any of his ex-players did well elsewhere, especially as, we were always willing to acknowledge him as the godfather, the guy who had taught us all we knew. I don't think he wanted any of us to be successful while he was still managing.

A few weeks after I had contacted big Jock about Brian McLaughlin, Dundee were drawn away to Celtic in the opening round of the 1978 Scottish Cup. I thought I had discovered a way to outfox big Jock, whom I would be confronting as a rival manager for the first time. About three weeks before the game, I booked the Seamill Hydro, Celtic's habitual haunt before key matches, and reserved its rooms for the Thursday and Friday nights before the Saturday when the match was scheduled to go ahead at Celtic Park. That had thwarted big Jock's plan to have his team stay in their usual pre-match surroundings. We went down to Seamill on the arranged date, our preparations were going well and I thought that at last I had got one over on big Jock. Then I got a phone call from big Jock on that January Friday morning: 'I think you'd better come up and see the park. It has iced up.' He had had the hoses out and had flooded the park on the Thursday so that it would ice up overnight. The game had no chance of going ahead on the Saturday. Jock got the referee in on the Friday afternoon, the game was called off and on the Saturday morning we headed back up to Dundee. That was him getting one back on me. The rearranged fixture was due on Monday of the following week so I asked the directors, who had quite enjoyed their stay at Seamill, if we could stay there again in advance of the rescheduled tie. They gave me the green light but when I phoned Seamill I discovered that Jock had already booked the Hydro for Celtic. There was no happy ending on the park either: they beat us 7–1. He got the last laugh, as so often before.

I was lucky at Dundee in that when I started out as manager they had only three directors: Graham Thomson, the managing director of Timex; Willie Lyburn, a farmer from Blairgowrie; and Ian Gellatly, the chairman, an accountant. If I wished to discuss a matter concerning money, I wouldn't go to the chairman; I would go to Graham Thomson, outline the issue and ask him to have a word with Willie Lyburn. Graham Thomson would phone me back half an hour later, say that he had had a word with Willie and that Willie was quite agreeable. The next time a board meeting was called, I would put the issue on the agenda and Willie Lyburn and Graham Thomson would vote in my favour. The reason for going to them first was that when it came to financial matters, the chairman was always against spending money. It would not matter how good the reasons were or what the purpose of the outlay was; even if it was vital. It was best, therefore, to ensure that the outcome was a *fait accompli*.

If the matter I wished to bring up at a board meeting was to do with the playing side of things, such as a swop, I would go to the chairman, who tended to be amenable if the matter did not involve cash. He would usually be happy to go along with my suggestion so I would say to him, 'Would you have a wee word with Willie?' Half an hour later the chairman would phone me back to say that Willie was in agreement. They would call a board meeting, I would bring the matter up and the two of them would vote in favour of my idea. So I was always playing two against one. It wasn't exactly manipulation; maybe more like strategic manoeuvring. I would always have very good reasons for my suggestions but I could not do anything of note without going through the board and, although I knew more than them about the game and what was needed on the football side, they had to be given their say. Some diplomacy was necessary on my part to oil the decision-making wheels, but I always managed to get my own way, more or less, as far as board decisions were concerned. I had a good relationship with the directors and before raising any issue with them I tried to think myself into their shoes and work out how they would react to what I was putting forward.

We missed promotion by a whisker at the end of my first season as manager. Morton and Hearts went up to the Premier Division after both had finished on 58 points, and we had finished on 57. We had scored more goals, 91, than either of them and had a better goal difference but that counted for nothing in the end. It was very tight at the top of the First Division. My second season as manager ended with us winning the 1978–79 First Division title but we finished only one point ahead of Kilmarnock, who were also promoted, and Clydebank, who were behind Kilmarnock only on goal difference.

The hardest thing in football is to step up a division and survive. You build a side that is good enough to play in a lower division but then, almost overnight, you require a brand new side. You need a different type of player for the top division. Work-rate, fight and 'dig' are the qualities you look for in First Division players but those qualities will only take you so far at the top end of the Scottish game. We knew, once we had won promotion, that we needed to get in some guys with more skill and ability but we didn't have any money and, when we tried to arrange swop deals for players, the other managers were not really interested. Willie Wallace and I went all over England and Scotland trying to get players but clubs wanted money, not swops, and we didn't have any. Even if a club agreed to a swop, the deal often hit a snag over the signing fee that Dundee would be offering to the player in question. That fee could be as little as £3,000 but Dundee would want to pay it to the player in three equal instalments over the length of his contract. Players, though, would often want the entire fee up front, and a number of deals collapsed because Dundee did not have the money to lay out immediately on signing a player. I always tried to encourage the players whom I was bringing to Dens Park to try to get money from the club they were leaving, but when I was swopping players and they asked me what Dundee would give them on leaving, I could offer them nothing. The only incentive I could hold out was the chance to get a good signing fee from the club to which they were going. That's how tight things were financially.

We had a squad of good, honest professionals but we found, on reaching the Premier Division, that we were being overrun in midfield. As a solution we bulked out the midfield by playing defensive midfielders. That went some way to preventing the opposition playing their game but it reduced our own contribution to a match because it meant there was less creativity in our side. We were creating fewer chances and scoring fewer goals.

I ran into George Best once again during that 1979–80 season. George, who had joined Hibs in late 1979, had undergone an operation to have implants sewn into his stomach to combat his alcoholism; if he drank, the alcohol would react with those implants to make him sick. I had got to know him quite well by this time, having met him whilst playing in a number of testimonial matches. So when he came up to Dens Park with Hibs to play against Dundee I invited him into my office after the match. I briefly forgot he had had these implants inserted and said to him, 'George, what would you like to drink?' The words had no sooner left my mouth than I realised what I had done. I said, 'Sorry about that, George.' He said, 'I'll have a vodka and tonic.' At that time he was training down south, then flying up to Edinburgh on Thursday night to train with the team on Friday morning. That would not prevent him drinking: he would go out in Edinburgh on the Thursday and Friday nights. He was being paid serious money by Hibs: £2,000 per match, which was very good money in the late 70s. That was because he had the potential to double Hibs' gates. It was similar to Dundee's deal with Jimmy Johnstone – and Bestie, like Jimmy, quickly blew his deal.

We did severe damage to Celtic's hopes of winning the League title when we met them at Dens Park in early April 1980. I knew that if we allowed them the time and space to knock the ball around in the middle of the park they would destroy us so I devised a means of stopping them playing while simultaneously providing us with an attacking advantage. I had signed a forward called Ian Fleming from Sheffield Wednesday – he had previously played for Aberdeen – and he was a sturdy, stocky wee guy; sharp, tenacious and good in the air. He worked hard, could win the ball and turned out to be a good player for Dundee. On the Tuesday morning at training before that Celtic match, I asked him if he fancied playing in central midfield on the Saturday. He said, 'Boss, I've never played in midfield in my life.' I said, 'I'll tell you what I want you to do: I want you to go into the middle of midfield and shut down Celtic's midfield with your tackling and win the ball for us. That's when Celtic have the ball. When we have the ball at the back and the ball is knocked forward, I want you to use your ability in the air to knock the ball on to the front players to support them.' I wasn't asking him to do anything he could not do: all I was asking of him was to do the same things in midfield as he normally did up front. I told our defenders that when they had the ball at the back they were to send it towards Fleming, and I told our forwards that they were not to drop off the front line to try to win balls that were played forward. That would leave Fleming free to do his stuff and set up our attackers.

We suffered an early fright when Roy Aitken, the Celtic midfield player, opened the scoring after seven minutes but gradually our tactics began to work and Iain Ferguson obtained an early equaliser for Dundee. Ferguson, who would go on to play for Rangers and Hearts, had just turned eighteen but he was our nominated penalty taker because he was close to flawless in hitting the net from the spot. At 1–1, and midway through the first half, we were awarded a penalty kick and I said to Willie Wallace, 'Now we'll find out what he is made of.' Ferguson, nerveless, smacked the ball right into the roof of the net. After that, we completely outplayed Celtic through controlling the middle of the park, which meant that we got a lot of the ball and could get balls to the front players. The goals came very easily and wee Fleming did a great job in midfield. He scored our third goal; Eric Sinclair made it 4–1; and Peter Mackie made it 5–1. Our plan had worked to perfection. We were 5–1 up with twenty minutes to go and we looked as though we could score a goal with every attack. Every time we crossed the halfway line Billy McNeill, the Celtic manager, and John Clark, his assistant, had their heads in their hands. Billy's face was like thunder at the end of that match.

Celtic had been leading the League for much of that season but they eventually lost the title by one point to Aberdeen. We were relegated along with Hibs so, good as that result against Celtic was, it did not help me in the end. Our players had lifted their game to play Celtic and we had been on a high after that victory but they could not keep up that form for the remainder of our fixtures. You would think that a team that had beaten Celtic 5–1 wouldn't have any problem avoiding relegation but it wasn't to be.

Wheeling and dealing and carrying out swop deals can only take you so far in football, especially at Premier Division level, and our lack of quality had been exposed at the top level. There was never enough money available at Dens Park to buy top-quality players so we were constantly juggling threadbare resources. The players would lift their games for local derbies and for matches against the Old Firm but in less highly charged matches, against more moderate opposition, their performances would for some reason drop a bit. You would have thought they were different players. Willie and I and Hughie Robertson (my other coach) used all the experience we had to vary the training and the approach to different things; sometimes it worked, sometimes it didn't. We got some good results in the Premier Division but we were not consistent enough and when the chips were down we failed to dig out results. The main problem was that we simply did not have enough players who were able to compete at the top level in Scotland. We had actually done rather well to stave off relegation until it was confirmed at the very end of the season and we got one or two notable results other than that 5–1 victory over Celtic. Hibs, who took the tumble into the First Division along with Dundee, were relegated long before we were.

Relegation inevitably signalled my dismissal as manager but there was no animosity between me and the directors when it came to the parting of the ways. I realised that everything was determined by results and even a 5–1 hiding of Celtic paled into insignificance when set against the season's overall results. I was not happy to lose my job but I could look back on two tremendous seasons in the First Division and having made a fair fist of our stay in the Premier Division. It was also in some ways a relief to get out of football management because I had become disillusioned by the demands and stresses of not having adequate resources to do justice to my abilities as a manager. My involvement with professional football was at an end – or so I thought.

10. A REALITY CHECK

A tumult of thoughts churned through my head as I sat in my car outside the social security office in Maryhill and pondered whether to enter its doors. Here was I, Tommy Gemmell, a man who had scored goals in two European Cup finals, contemplating whether to sign on the dole. Some people are unlucky enough to have no choice but to sign on, but they at least are able to do so anonymously. I knew that it would be different for me. As soon as I entered the doors of that office in Garrioch Road I would be setting off a chain of events that would lead to stories in the papers first thing the following morning of Tommy Gemmell, Celtic's European Cup star and former Scotland international, signing on. It was a gut-wrenching thought as I looked back on a football career that had shaped me into the man I was and given me two decades of memories and an exceptionally good living. It had also cost me my marriage and left me stranded in my late thirties without income or means of support.

Football management had put a lot of pressure on my marriage. The dual duties of managing Dundee Football Club and running my hotel in Errol had led to a lot of friction with Anne. It had been easy enough to run the hotel when I was a Dundee footballer because I could finish training and be back at the hotel by lunchtime to greet the regular drinkers who formed my hard-core clientele. Things became different when I entered the managerial side of the game. I spent a lot of time travelling to look at players and watch evening matches. As a manager, you never know where you are going to be in two days' time; you are always likely to have to go to see a player or perform some other duty at short notice.

Even on a normal day at the club, I would work long hours. After the senior squad had done their day's training, I would have a look at the young players and there would often be an afternoon match on a weekday in one of the leagues in which our teams competed. On match day I would have to spend a large chunk of the day away from the hotel on one of its busiest days of the week. Every day, I would get up at seven o'clock to do the hotel paperwork. The combination of football commitments and hotel-related work produced a seventeen- or eighteen-hour day. That weighs you down and frays tempers. I was determined, though, not to sell the hotel because I had it in the back of my mind that every football manager eventually gets the sack, and if I got the sack and had sold the hotel I would be left without income. I saw it as a safety net.

Anne had had to juggle the responsibility of looking after the children with running the pub while I was away, although her mother had moved in with us to help her out. My son David was five when I was appointed Dundee's manager and my daughter Karen Michelle was nearly ten. Our marriage had been reasonably good but the friction caused by my double duties had seen it become taut with tension. Eventually, in the winter of 1979, we separated. Anne moved out of the hotel, taking the children with her, and bought a house in Hamilton with her mother. I would go down and see the kids every Thursday. Anne and I were *en route* to divorce.

My salary as manager had risen from £10,000 plus a car in 1977 to £12,000 in 1978 and, in the promotion year of 1979, it was upped to £15,000 plus a club car and a share of the bonuses. That was what I was earning when I was dismissed in 1980. I don't know whether that was a particularly good or bad salary for a manager but it had certainly been sufficient for my needs, especially with the car and with many of my expenses being met by the club. I still had the hotel in Errol and continued to run it until late 1980, when a guy from Fife offered to buy it and I did a deal to sell it to him for £59,500.

I had no thought of going back into football. I was heartily sick of the game by then because of the pressures of management, and returning to that job, I thought, would be the equivalent of inflicting brain damage on myself. Being a manager is fine when you are winning but it has a habit of kicking you in the teeth just when you do not expect it and through no fault of your own.

I had a new partner, Mary, by the time I left Dundee and we used a large amount of the proceeds from selling the Commercial Hotel to purchase a house for ourselves in Blanefield, a little village just north of Glasgow that would be handily situated if I managed to get a job in the city. We agreed that I would take a three-month break during which I would not do anything except a bit of work on making improvements to the house. It was most enjoyable but once that time was up, it became clear that our money was fast running out and that I needed to find work quickly. I made more than 50 applications for sales posts; I chose sales jobs because I figured that the name of Tommy Gemmell, former footballer and Lisbon Lion, might carry me a considerable distance and that my face and reputation would open doors for me. The recipients of those letters did not seem quite so sure of that and after six months of writing to people there was nothing doing. I then discovered for the first time in my adult life that when there is no money coming into a household, the money you do have does not take long to go out. By then it was late 1981 and that was when I told Mary that I was going up to the dole office in Maryhill, which was the nearest one to Blanefield, to sign on. That grim, faceless building in Garrioch Road made a stark contrast with the pretty village of Blanefield and emphasised the predicament in which I found myself. I sat outside the building in my car and after half an hour of pondering the consequences of signing on, I put the key back in the ignition, turned the car round and drove back to Blanefield. The money had not quite run out and, although things were becoming pretty tight, I decided to tough it out for a bit longer before taking that most drastic of steps. Mary had been sitting beside me in the car all the time I had been thinking over my options outside the dole office. She had never said a word to sway me one way or the other but as we were driving back, she said, 'I think you did the right thing.'

Two weeks later, Tom Ogilvie, a very good friend of mine and an entrepreneur who owned a building company in Stirling, asked me if I would like to run one of his hotels, the Lady of the Lake

11. A ROVERS ROLE

The directors of Albion Rovers were always primed and prepared to toast any success that might come the way of the Coatbridge club. The drinks cabinet inside the boardroom at the club's Cliftonhill ground was permanently crammed with every variety of tipple and, as soon as a bottle was drained, it was immediately replaced. It did not seem to matter to the directors that any significant success had eluded the club since the 40s, or that the drinks cabinet was about the only pristine part of a club whose stadium otherwise resembled nothing so much as a rat hole. Nor, in fact, did they require success as an excuse to break into that drinks cabinet – bottles were emptied and replaced on a frequent basis, even when the club was at rock bottom, which was more often than not.

Early in the new year of 1986 I had taken a phone call from Tam Fagan, the Albion Rovers chairman. I knew Tam from my Celtic days; he had been a real man about town during the 60s and 70s and he used to come into the Vesuvio restaurant in Glasgow at the time when it was one of the Celtic players' major haunts. Tam was a lovable rogue. He had a nightclub situated about 400 yards from Cliftonhill and it did good business, but he would come in with his girlfriend, open the till, help himself to the readies and not even leave a note to say how much he had removed. Not surprisingly, the place eventually took a nosedive. Tam had been the major shareholder in Rovers for years and he would just run rollercoaster over the other directors.

It was at tea-time on a Friday evening that Tam Fagan rang me. Albion Rovers didn't have a manager and they were playing

Queen's Park in the Scottish Cup the following day. He wanted me to take over in time for that tie. Tam had become unwell by the mid-'80s and could not get out and about very much. I had moved home from Blanefield to Uddingston by then and he lived only five minutes down the road so I went down to speak to him face to face. His house looked lovely from outside but inside it was an almost Dickensian picture of decay and decrepitude. Tam was sitting beside a big electric fire in the midst of it all. He was a heavy smoker and he had clearly fallen asleep on one occasion, either with a cigarette still burning or else with his arm too close to the fire, because the sleeve of the big, grey, polo-necked jumper that he was wearing had a massive hole with singe marks.

I asked Tam if the club had any money and he said no. I was still tempted to take the job but I told Tam I would do so only on the condition that I was given a free hand with regard to all playing matters. He wasn't sure about that but he eventually agreed. I emphasised that if there was any interference in playing matters at directorial level I would walk. I asked him what he would pay me and he again became a bit evasive. He clearly thought I would be looking for a sizeable salary based on my previous experience. We finally settled on the modest figure of £50 per week plus expenses. I became the club's 29th manager in 66 years; the manager of Albion Rovers changed almost as often as the prime minister of Italy.

I knew I was never going to be under any pressure in that job: Albion Rovers expect to get beaten every week anyway. So I was not putting my reputation on the line because Rovers could not do any worse than they were doing, so the only way was up. The job was convenient for me: Cliftonhill was only ten minutes up the road from my house in Uddingston. I would never have joined a club as manager if it had involved extensive travelling and managing Albion Rovers was going to be as intense a job as I had had at Dundee; in fact, it was almost as if I was giving myself a wee interest, a hobby. I had no delusions of grandeur and no aspirations to return to full-time football management.

I asked Mary, who was soon to become my wife, if she fancied coming along to our first match, away to Queen's Park in the Scottish Cup at Hampden Park. Mary hates football but I told her she would love attending a match at Hampden and it would give her a chance to meet the directors. We walked into the boardroom at Hampden and were immediately attended to by a waiter wearing a white jacket and pleated trousers, carrying a napkin on his arm and bearing a silver salver. 'Hello, Mr Gemmell,' he said, 'nice to see you again. Would you like a drink?' I ordered a gin and tonic and introduced Mary to both clubs' directors and their wives. As I left for the dressing room to give my first team talk, I could see Mary looking round the ornate Hampden boardroom and thinking that this was a side of football to which she could grow accustomed.

Albion Rovers played well that day and although we lost the cup tie to Queen's Park I thought I could see some potential among the players and was sure I could improve them further. I had been quite happy with their display. Joe Baker, the former Arsenal, Hibs and England forward, was assistant manager at Rovers and had filled that role for several years. He did not feel that being the manager would suit him and was quite happy to stay in the background. I could trust Joe fully – you couldn't find a more likeable guy. He had a good eye for a player and was a good reader of the game. He had filled me in in detail on the capabilities of all the players I was inheriting. They seemed to be fit enough but I got the impression that they had not been receiving a lot of help tactically or in other ways. I felt I could provide some input in that area and, although I was not treating the job with an enormous intensity, I still wanted to see signs on match days that the help I was giving them was bringing improvement to their football. Otherwise, there was little point in me being there. They lacked organisation in defence, midfield and up front and my task was to instil it.

Mary had been looked after very well during the Queen's Park match at Hampden. She had been provided with a tartan rug to help keep the cold at bay when she went out to watch the game, which took place amidst light snow showers, and she had enjoyed a tasty buffet at half-time. When I joined her in the boardroom shortly after the final whistle, we were given refreshments. It had all been very civilised. As we headed into Glasgow for dinner after the match, Mary said, 'That was great.' So I said to her, 'We're playing at Cliftonhill next week. Do you want to go?' She agreed to come along, so on the afternoon of my first home game as Rovers manager I took her into the boardroom at Cliftonhill. They offered her a drink and when they opened the cupboard that held the glasses, there was not one the same shape as any other. At half-time she offered to help with the tea and sandwiches and when she went to get the china, there wasn't a single cup or saucer that was without a chip in it. Despite the shambolic nature of their arrangements, they still managed to ply her with gin and tonics as often as she required them. Mary said to me on the way home, 'It's shocking in that kitchen: everything is filthy.' I said to her, 'If you think that's bad, you should see the dressing rooms.'

I had once played in a closed-doors friendly for Celtic against Albion Rovers at Cliftonhill and the pitch had been in fine condition but in the dressing room we had found six-inch nails hammered into the walls for coat pegs and the tiling in the bath had been chipped and dirty; it was a real health hazard. There hadn't even been a shower as an alternative to the bath. On my arrival as manager a decade and a half later, it didn't look any different, though there were real coat hooks on the walls instead of nails. We did not have enough balls for each player to get one in training. The towels were grotty, as was the training gear. The toilet in our dressing room didn't flush so they placed a plastic bucket full of water beside it and once someone had finished using the toilet, they were expected to use this bucket of water to flush the toilet, then fill it up for the next person to use. On matchday afternoons, when the toilet was used by almost every nervous player before the match, it was a sight to behold.

The environmental health people would have closed the kitchen at Cliftonhill if they had walked in and seen it. It was falling apart so when Mary's mother was changing her kitchen units I asked the chairman, Davie Forrester, if he would like the units for the ground. (Sadly, Tam Fagan's illness had taken its toll and he had passed away in the months since I had become manager.) Davie Forrester said, 'Oh, that would be great.' I said, 'She's looking for £50 for them.' He recoiled, saying, 'Oh, I don't know about that.' She eventually got her £50 but the units lay untouched inside Cliftonhill for months because, I was told, the club could not afford to get a joiner to install them. Eventually they got somebody – I think it was one of the supporters – to carry out the work.

The club used a red-ash pitch for training in the Whifflet district of Coatbridge. It would be littered with empty Buckfast bottles, broken glass and beer cans every time we turned up for a training session, but despite the dreadful facilities, the club did have some reasonable players, such as a guy called Tony Gallagher, who was captain and played at centre-half. Alan Rodgers was a tidy midfield player and and a black guy who played wide on the right up front, called Victor Kasule, also had ability. I also brought in Allen McKnight, a big goalkeeper from Northern Ireland, on loan from Celtic.

Kasule could really play but he was an insolent individual and I always had to keep a very close eye on him. On one match day, an Albion Rovers director came to me about an hour before kick-off and told me that someone had just seen Victor Kasule in a local pub. I told Joe Baker to get up to the pub and get Kasule down to the ground immediately. On his arrival I asked him what he thought he was doing. All the supporters would go into that pub to have a drink before the match so if Kasule was sitting among them an hour before kick-off it did not look as if he was taking his duties particularly seriously, especially if he was having a drink. He told me that he had only been drinking orange juice and he didn't think he was doing any harm. I made it clear to him that it wasn't to happen again.

Kasule saw himself as Mr Glamorous of Albion Rovers. He fancied himself with the birds and thought he was above the other players, so he had to be cut down to size frequently. One day at Arbroath he pushed me so far that I had him by the throat and was ready to take a swing at him. We were winning the match, there were two or three minutes to go and Kasule received the ball on the right and began trying to nutmeg other players. If he went past a defender and left him on the ground, he would turn back and wave at him to humiliate him. He had stopped playing for the team and instead was trying to tease the opposition to show how big a player he was. I said to Joe Baker, 'Get him off the park.' Joe said, 'There are only a couple of minutes to go.' I said, 'Get him off' – even though we had used up all our substitutes. We brought him off the park and, as he was going up the Gayfield players' tunnel I followed him, grabbed him by the throat and pushed him against the wall. His big eyes were almost popping out of his skull. I said, 'Don't you dare treat your fellow professionals like that.' I was just about to swing for him when Joe Baker got his hands round me and stopped me. You don't mind players wasting time professionally but when they start abusing other players you have to draw the line.

Kasule was a good player, with considerable ability, pace and a big long stride, and that combination enabled him to go past players at will, but because of his attitude I used to leave him out of the team now and then. I did manage to get him to play reasonably consistently, which had not been happening before I arrived. He lived in Glasgow and had been in the habit of going out on a Friday night – I knew all about that because I had received a couple of phone calls about it. So I said to him, 'I'm going to get someone to follow you from your house to see where you go.' That helped to tone down his behaviour because he had no other job than playing for Albion Rovers so he needed the money he was getting from football, even though that did not amount to much, maybe around £30 a week plus expenses. I don't know why he was so wayward because he was from a very respectable background: his father was a surgeon and his mother a headmistress.

By the time I had been their manager for a couple of years, Albion Rovers had become a confident, well-drilled, well-organised, fit, competent side, in such a healthy condition that they were even poised nicely to make a bit of a push for the promotion places. Once players get into a habit of winning matches they don't want to get out of it, and if you are a lower division team and you are organised, then you are halfway there. Albion had been struggling at the bottom of the Second Division when I had joined them in early 1986 and I had not been able to turn things around quickly enough to prevent them finishing second from bottom at the end of that 1985–86 season, but we finished eighth in the Second Division in 1986–87, Rovers' best position for eight years.

Davie Forrester was a chartered accountant and he became alarmed when some success developed during my time as manager because it meant that the players started to receive regular bonuses, something that hadn't often happened before. One day he said to me, 'We can't afford to keep paying these bonuses.' I said, 'Too bad, Davie. It's in their contracts that they get a certain amount for a win and a certain amount for a draw and that was sorted out before the season started.' He said, 'The bank manager has been on to me about it.' I thought, Oh no, this is shades of Dundee. I am not going to have to contend with another bank manager. So the club had to begin branching out to raise some extra funds. We obtained shirt sponsors and, for the first time, Albion Rovers replica jerseys became available to supporters. We encouraged local businessmen to sponsor matches at a cost of £1,200, in return for which their dozen-strong party received lunch at a local hotel, drinks in the boardroom, a presentation of some crystal glasses and twelve seats in the stand. I arranged for five or six of my business contacts to take pity on this Cinderella team and help us out. I always made sure I targeted guys who enjoyed a refreshment because one thing was for sure at Albion Rovers: you would never be short of a drink in the boardroom. I remember we had a board meeting one night that finished at half past eight and I never got out of the boardroom until after eleven o'clock. Once all business had been attended to, the bevvy was broken into with a vengeance.

The one thing I had failed to realise before taking the job was the amount of work that would be involved. I was on the phone in my office at Abbey Life for at least an hour and a half to two hours every day on club business; then there were the two training nights and the match day. After almost two years as Rovers manager, in December 1987, I decided to resign because of business pressures. I was managing an office for Abbey Life but because of my football work I was beginning to neglect aspects of my daily work and that could not continue.

On my departure Albion Rovers were sitting seventh in the Second Division, which I regarded as a notable achievement at a club that had made only the scantiest of resources available to me during my time as manager. It had been good fun because we had won quite a lot of matches and played reasonably good football. It got to the point where the directors and supporters were expecting a victory in every game after years in which they hadn't been used to winning. Rovers would go on to win their first promotion for 40 years in the season after I left the club. I like to think that something must have rubbed off on them from my time there.

It had been interesting to deal with the players at Rovers. You had good, honest players there who would work their backsides off for you and you also had players whose idiosyncrasies prevented them ever making the leap to a higher level. One of our forwards was a tall, wiry guy who could score tremendous goals from twenty yards but if he was presented with the ball two yards out from goal he would send it over the bar. He had the awareness and ability to get into good positions inside the penalty area but his finishing from close-range was awful. Tam Fagan had managed to make it along to the first couple of matches in which this player featured and after the second occasion he told me, 'I'll not be back to any matches in which he is playing.' I played the boy in every game and if I was ever wavering about whether to include him, I remembered the chairman's words. So we never saw the chairman at any matches and I must say that that hadn't particularly upset me.

I had had no further involvement in football when, in April 1993, I was asked to return to Albion Rovers. The club was back in its old ways: three managers had been in charge in the little more than five years since I had left and Rovers were rooted to bottom spot in the Second Division. I got a phone call from Jack McGoogan, who had succeeded Davie Forrester as chairman, asking me if I would like to go back. I saw him and went through the same rigmarole as I had with Tam Fagan. Nothing had changed: the club was still short of money, but we sorted out a financial arrangement under which I would be paid £100 per week and I agreed to take on the job for a second spell.

When I saw the players they now had at the club, I was shocked. Some of them could not pass a ball ten or fifteen yards. I had brought in Andy Lynch, the former Celtic full-back, as my assistant, and on the first night of training with Albion Rovers we looked at each other quizzically because the players were what you might describe as being very much less than ordinary. We tried to get them organised but it was an uphill struggle. Then

McGoogan started making noises about what I should and shouldn't do with the team. I had to remind him that when we had first met in his office he had said there would be no interference from him in playing matters. Things had quickly begun to look ominous.

We suffered a severe early setback when, on 11 August 1993, we faced a Premier Division side, Partick Thistle, in a League Cup tie. It was a home game for us but had to be moved to Fir Park, Motherwell, to accommodate the unusually large crowd for a Rovers match: even though the attendance only amounted to around 1,500, that was five times greater than our usual gate for home Second Division matches. It was a strange game: after the opening 25 minutes we could have been three goals ahead and it was still reasonably tight at half-time – Thistle were 2–0 up, which wasn't too bad considering they were two divisions higher than us. Then, in the second half, they overran us and we collapsed. We made mistakes at the back, they went further ahead and soon our players had given up; the midfield went to pieces, the defence disintegrated and Thistle could have scored a goal every time they attacked. We had fallen apart completely by the end and it finished 11–1 to Partick Thistle. There was nothing I could say or do after that match. It was a disaster. It remains Albion Rovers' record defeat.

Shortage of cash meant that I could not bring in players to replace those that had been there on my arrival. We badly needed a centre-half so I gave a trial to an eighteen-year-old youngster whom I had had recommended to me, and who played for an amateur club in the Dumbarton area. I played him in two reserve matches and he was better than what we had despite having come from amateur football. I was sufficiently impressed to phone him up and ask him to play in a midweek match for the first team. He agreed to turn out for us and I told him to ask his amateur club's secretary to accompany him to the game. I urgently required players and I was so convinced he would do well enough for our first team that I knew I would probably want to sign him after the match. If his club secretary was present, we might be able to do a deal on the spot to obtain his signature.

He went out and played very well so after the match I asked the amateur club's secretary for a word in my office to see what sort of money they were looking for as compensation for the boy. He said, 'Two hundred pounds.' The directors knew I was going to make an approach for the player so when I went back into the boardroom, I said, 'The young boy wants to sign for us. What did you think of the way he played?' They agreed that he had done well so I told them that we needed to pay £200 compensation to his club if we were to sign him. There was a collective sharp intake of breath. 'We don't have £200,' was the response. I said, 'What? You don't have £200? You've got a fucking booze cupboard full to the gunnels; you couldn't get another bottle in it. There'll be more than £200 worth of booze in there.' From that point, the board of directors and I started drifting apart.

If that was not enough to show me the board's attitude to financing the club, the message was hammered home when we went to play a match away to Alloa Athletic at Recreation Park a week before Christmas 1993. I was now living in Dunblane and Alloa was only a fifteen-minute drive from my house so I decided to travel directly to the ground. I phoned wee Jimmy Lawson, who did everything behind the scenes at Albion Rovers: he washed the strips, looked after the boots and maintained the pitch. I told Jimmy to wait at Cliftonhill until I had seen the pitch at Alloa so that I could tell him what type of studs to put in the boots. Shortly after I arrived at Recreation Park, the referee went out to inspect the field of play. One corner of the pitch was awash with water. The referee threw the ball up in the air inside the centre circle and watched it drop on to the turf and land stone dead; that is how heavy the pitch had become after a day of incessant rain. The referee, incredibly, decided he would let the game go ahead as long as the corner of the ground that was under water could be cleared. I thought to myself, Well . . . long studs today. I phoned Jimmy Lawson and told him to change all the studs in the boots to the longest studs he had. He replied, 'We haven't got any long studs.' I could not believe it but I had to act quickly as kick-off was only a couple of hours away. I told him to take all the studs out of the boots and get to Alloa about fifteen or twenty minutes earlier than he normally would for an away match. I then went chasing around Alloa to find a sports shop and was lucky enough to eventually to find one in which I bought sixteen sets of long studs. They cost £17.50. Later I went into the boardroom at Alloa and said to Robin Marwick, a Rovers official, 'There is the receipt for the studs.' He said, 'Oh, we can't give you that.' I said, 'That is a necessary expense incurred by me on behalf of the club.' I could not believe that the directors would contemplate refusing to pay me back. I eventually received the money but only after a month and I felt it was given grudgingly. That was one of various episodes that showed me how little ambition there was at Albion Rovers.

One evening in January 1994 I had a meeting with the directors in the boardroom which lasted from around seven o'clock to after eleven. The discussion was centred on how the club was going to improve the playing staff by getting new players in to replace the ones we had and the exchanges became more and more heated. I pointed out how they had denied me the £200 required to bring in a centre-half and said that if I was to use that as a benchmark, then the chances of improving the playing staff were very slim indeed. If you've got bad players and you can't get them out and put better players in, where do you go from there? Eventually, I told them that they should go their way and I would go mine and that was the end of my Albion Rovers saga.

12. AFTER THE GAME

It was while taking a week's golfing holiday without golf clubs in Majorca that I first met Mary. Bertie Auld, a couple of pals and Bertie's brother were with me that spring of 1977. I intended to hire clubs once we had pitched up on the Spanish island but I never played at all. Mary had been working in Majorca as a nanny to the children of some friends of hers who ran a bar in Magaluf and that is where I met her: in the pub one lunchtime. I noticed her when she walked in wearing only a bikini. She didn't know who I was because she does not come from a football background at all although she is from the East End of Glasgow.

Following my return to Scotland, we kept in touch through phone calls. Later in 1977, after I had become Dundee's manager, the club did not have any fixtures in a ten-day period so the directors agreed that I could go for another week's golfing holiday in Majorca. That allowed Mary and me the opportunity to get to know each other a bit better. She would come home every three months or so to visit her parents and we would meet in Glasgow. She eventually came back for good and I would get together with her once a fortnight. My marriage, it was clear to me, was crumbling, but I would stress that Mary had nothing to do with the break-up; that was all to do with the tension surrounding our running the Commercial Hotel. To the best of my knowledge, Anne did not even know that Mary had become part of my life when she left the hotel in Errol in the winter of 1979.

Anne and I had been separated from that point but divorce proceedings didn't start until 1985. Once I had found a good lawyer, in early 1986, who could see the matter through, he promised to complete the entire process within six weeks and he was as good as his word. I had to take the divorce papers to Anne myself to get her signature, and we agreed on access to the children and the financial settlement. Within three days of the decree nisi, Mary said, 'Let's get married.' I said, 'Why not?' I had no second thoughts because we had been living together since the second half of 1980 and had known each other for three years before that. We had got on so well during those nine years that it seemed natural to get married. Before I knew it, Mary had arranged everything. We were married at the registry office at Giffnock, on the south side of Glasgow, in May 1986, and had 25 guests to a late lunch at the Bothwell Bridge Hotel. Tom Ogilvie, my best man, his wife, Mary and I went up for a couple of nights at Gleneagles, where a pal of ours had two apartments in the grounds. Mary and I then went off on honeymoon, flying to Dubrovnik on Croatia's Dalmatian Coast and sailing from there to a different Greek island every day for a week before docking in Athens.

Mary is down to earth. She is not a poser; she doesn't go out and say, 'Look at my dress.' She is a straightforward Glaswegian lassie with the same type of humour as I have, a smashing wife and a smashing cook. She has a great personality and looks great – she is a cracker. There is an age difference – she is nine years younger than me – but that has never been a problem. Once we were married, we did think about having children and talked about it quite a bit but eventually Mary said, 'If we have any kids, then by the time they are in their early twenties, you will be in your middle sixties.' She didn't think that a youngster of that age should have a father of retirement age. I told her to think long and hard about it because that would not have bothered me one bit. I left it as her decision and the next thing I knew she had booked me into a clinic in Glasgow for 'the snip'. We have never had any regrets about not having kids and Mary is a tremendous auntie to her nieces and nephews and a loving stepmother to my children.

Office life, and starting a new career in my forties, as a financial adviser, proved to be quite a contrast after my hectic days in football and looking after a hotel and a pub. Mary and I had been doing an eighteen-hour day, six days a week, whilst running the

Lady of the Lake in Bridge of Allan and going from that to an eight-hour day with Abbey Life in the mid-80s was like heaven. The only slight drawback was that during the early 80s we had moved from Blanefield to a cottage in Cambusbarron, near Stirling, so there was quite a lot of travelling involved in going to and from Glasgow. Mary by then had a job in Glasgow in advertising telesales with Yellow Pages, at which she excelled because she is a great communicator, so we would travel to Glasgow together. It was so good to be able to go home with one another at tea-time, have a bite to eat, put our feet up and watch the telly. Nevertheless, the extensive daily travelling from Cambusbarron to Glasgow gave us reason to move to Uddingston in the mid-80s. We had a nice three-bedroom villa, Mary's sister and parents lived within a ten-minute drive and it was handier for the office. It wasn't long before we were half-thinking of moving again because our house was being used by visitors as if it was bed-and-breakfast lodgings. We had a patio with a barbecue and I had a lot of colleagues and friends who lived near me, so almost every weekend we would either have visitors in the house or a barbecue outside. It got to the stage that we never had a weekend to ourselves. One day, we were invited up to Stirling for lunch by Tom Ogilvie, who owned D & J Ogilvie, a big building company there. When we mentioned that we had had thoughts of moving he took us round three of the sites on which his firm was building. One of them, in Dublane, was a set of apartments that were being constructed around an old stone-worked mill. The only way they could get planning permission to build apartments on that land was to renovate the mill using the same stone as had been used in the original building. It was to be part of a complex that contained a swimming pool and sauna and was situated right on a river bank. The apartment Tom showed us was exactly the right size for us and had only one spare bedroom, so the largest number we can have to stay at the weekend is a couple, which makes things a lot more peaceful than they were in Uddingston. We moved into the apartment in March 1989 and have been living there ever since.

As a manager at Dundee, I had had to undertake only a very light amount of elementary paperwork: the bulk of it, the heavy stuff, had been done by the club secretary. It was very different when I joined Abbey Life and found that I had to complete several hours of paperwork a day. That bored me rigid because both in football and in running a pub I had been on the go all the time. Sitting at a desk doing paperwork drove me crazy. It never put me off being a financial consultant because I was enjoying it and was making a few quid with Abbey Life, who in the 80s were the top company in the business of selling life insurance, mortgages and pensions.

The hardest thing, as a financial adviser, is to get started. My way of doing so was through contacting all the guys I had got to know in my football days for whom I had arranged match tickets down the years. I would phone them up and say, 'Remember those tickets I got for you . . . ?' I blackmailed them, essentially, into doing some business with me. Once I had got started and knew the system I became quite successful and there is no doubt that being Tommy Gemmell, former footballer, has helped me. I make no apologies for using my name as a door-opener to attract business. The longer it works, the better.

I have done all right in this business: I have been to a sales convention with every company I have worked for, and you qualify to attend a convention only if you achieve your sales targets. The venues for the conventions I have attended have ranged from Florida to Paris to the Caribbean for a cruise. The cruise on the *Sea Princess* which Mary and I used as our honeymoon was actually part of an Abbey Life convention. I must have been doing something right to have been included in all those conventions. No expense was spared on them in the past but now all the companies are tightening their belts because almost all of them are listed on the stockmarket and are therefore answerable to their shareholders.

I remained with Abbey Life from 1983 to 1987, becoming a group manager after three years. I spearheaded a group of 25 people and was in charge of recruitment and training sessions. On top of my income from the sales I made, I was receiving a percentage of what the other guys made. That did make for a slightly longer working day, maybe a 12-hour day sometimes, but because my income was boosted by that promotion I didn't mind that too much. I was then headhunted by Imperial Trident Life and stayed there for two and a half years as an office manager before switching to Sun Life. After six years at Sun Life, I moved in the mid-90s to a company called GAN Financial Services. Each time I moved I was headhunted, which indicates again that I can't have been doing too badly. GAN were a French company, 49 per cent-owned by the French government. Things were fine and dandy until they decided they wanted to float on the French stockmarket; to do so, under French regulations, they had to divest their shares in their UK company. All the guys I worked with at GAN joined Royal Sun Alliance when GAN pulled out of Britain in the late 90s and, after a couple of years, we were all headhunted by Park Row Associates, a company of independent financial advisers whose three founding directors had been with GAN in London. I remain in the Glasgow office of Park Row Associates, whose head office is in Leeds.

My name does get me in the door as a financial adviser but it doesn't get me the business. I've got to convince people of the benefits of taking certain courses of action financially and our compliance department is like the Gestapo: if you don't adhere to the regulations when dealing with the public, you are soon out of the door. Compliance is a very important aspect of our business because we are regulated directly by the Financial Services Authority and our compliance people check our files to ensure we will not upset the FSA. They will visit unannounced, pull out six of my files, go through them with a fine-tooth comb and then pull me in and ask me, in rigorous detail, why I carried out a particular sale in a particular way, stressing the importance of documenting every reason for every action in every sale. Everything nowadays has to be done in such a way as to prove to the FSA that with every sale you did the utmost to ensure that the client was given the best possible deal available to someone in their particular circumstances. I am pleased to say that I have not had one complaint made against me in the 21 years in which I have been a financial adviser.

During the mid-90s, following my second stint as manager of Albion Rovers, I augmented my work as a financial adviser with a spell at Radio Clyde. Davie Provan, the former Celtic footballer who works at Radio Clyde, phoned me and said that Radio Clyde wanted to freshen things up and bring in some new people to do updates from matches as they took place on a Saturday afternoon. They were also bringing in simultaneously Terry Butcher, the ex-Rangers and England centre-back, and David Syme, the former referee. I said I would be interested; I didn't see any reason not to do it. I would go to a match and provide regular bulletins throughout the afternoon, mainly on home matches for Hibs, Hearts, Dunfermline Athletic and Raith Rovers because those clubs' grounds were within easy reach of Dunblane. It was good fun doing that for a couple of seasons. It was also a wee bit hair-raising at times because at some grounds the press box is away at the back of the stand and it isn't always easy to make out the players. It is very difficult, for example, to make out the number on the back of the pinstriped Dunfermline Athletic jersey and you could be put on the spot when a goal was scored and you had to identify the goal scorer right away, on air. So the old ticker would be thumping away as I tried to compose myself and broadcast the nuts and bolts of what had happened to the waiting audience. It was still a quite enjoyable way to pass Saturday afternoons for a couple of years.

I see more of my son David now than I did when he was growing up. He looks after leisure facilities at a school in Stirling, works as a coach at Stirling Albion and does some coaching for the Scottish Football Association at different schools. He began coaching the Stirling Albion under-16s, then the under-19s and then helped out with the first team. Once Allan Moore was appointed head coach of Stirling Albion in the summer of 2002, he made David his assistant and they won promotion from the third division in 2004. My daughter, Karen Michelle, is married and lives down in Doncaster and she is in charge of a team at a call centre. So the two of them are doing all right. Karen Michelle's first job was actually as a stable girl in Jimmy Fitzgerald's racing stable in Malton, Yorkshire, when she left school at sixteen and she lived in digs at the stable. My former wife, Anne, then decided to uproot David from Hamilton and move down to Malton – so that was David in another school. Mary and I would drive down to Malton three or four times a year, stay in a hotel, and see the kids. I have always got on very well with both of them. Karen Michelle came to live with us in Dunblane for four years before going south again and David came up seven years ago and lived with us for five years, then lived in digs for a year and a half before, in the autumn of 2003, moving into his own flat in Dunblane. People don't stay with you for that length of time if they are not very keen on you and they get on great with Mary. I have to say that I am proud of the way in which David and Karen Michelle have developed into decent young people.

My mementoes of my career in football remained with me until the '90s, when I decided it was time to part company with them. I gave the Internazionale shirt that I had exchanged with Sandro Mazzola at the National Stadium in Lisbon in 1967 to the Lisbon Lions committee to auction for charity on the 25th anniversary of our European Cup win. They stuck it in a frame and I think they got around £6,500 for it. I also had my medals auctioned at Christie's in Glasgow during the mid-'90s and Willie Haughey, the Glasgow entrepreneur, bought them. He generously allowed them to be mounted in a beautiful frame, and they now hang on the wall inside the boardroom at Celtic Park along with those of Jimmy Johnstone: a pleasant contrast to their previous resting place, a polythene bag at the bottom of our bedroom wardrobe. I couldn't insure the medals because nobody would insure them unless I put them in a bank vault and there is not much point insuring something only to stick it in a bank vault. They had almost been lost to me for good when Mary and I were living in Uddingston during the late '80s and were burgled. The medals had been hanging in a frame of our own in the dining room, but the thieves overlooked them. That incident helped me decide to sell them and the proceeds – £33,000 – went straight into my pension fund.

The first major reunion of the Lisbon Lions was in 1988, celebrating the 21st anniversary of the European Cup win. Although we had always kept in touch before that, it was only after we had all retired from the management and coaching side of football that we started to get together more regularly. During the '90s, corporate hospitality on match days at Celtic Park would be hosted by Lisbon Lions such as myself, Bobby Lennox, Stevie Chalmers, Ronnie Simpson, Bobby Murdoch, Billy McNeill and

Bertie Auld. When we went into corporate boxes to meet Celtic supporters, you could see people's faces lighting up. The affection that Celtic supporters still had for the Lisbon Lions was quite incredible. It was good to know that though we were gone, we were not forgotten.

The Lions seem to be more in demand now than ever before. With every year that passes, the singularity of our achievement in winning the European Cup grows greater. The fans also appreciate that we remain accessible to them and have time for them. Mary finds it strange that youngsters who never saw me play ask me to sign Celtic jerseys for them. Being a Lisbon Lion means that I always have to be prepared for people to approach me about the feats of 25 May 1967. Once, Mary and I were on holiday in Portugal and were in a bar having lunch and enjoying a bottle of wine. The rain was pouring so hard that rivulets were flowing down the street. This wee man was running past, getting soaked to the skin, but as he passed by he looked into the pub where we were sitting. He then turned back, stopped, came in and stood there soaking. He was a Scotsman on holiday. He said, 'Tommy Gemmell? Tommy, how are you doing? Do you remember me?' I could not quite place him so I said, 'Refresh my memory.' He said, 'Lisbon – you were in a traffic jam on the way to the final and my bus pulled up alongside the team bus and I was the one that waved at you.' He was deadly serious. We had him join us for a couple of drinks and for a long time after that he sent Mary and me Christmas cards.

I am honorary president of the Caithness Celtic Supporters' Club so Mary and I go up there every year for a supporters' rally; in 2004, for example, there were 190 people at the function in a beautiful hotel halfway between Thurso and Scrabster. I am president of the Luxembourg Celtic Supporters' Club and of the Derry Celtic Supporters' Club and we go to each of those places every year for a long weekend, all expenses paid by the supporters. We were guests of the Hong Kong Celtic Supporters' Club for ten days and were in Dubai for eight days as guests of the Celtic Supporters' Club in that country at the beginning of 2004. Mary and I will also have a couple of long weekends in London to ourselves and will go away on holiday a couple of times a year. So we enjoy a good spread of breaks.

On visiting a Celtic supporters' club, you do a bit of speechifying, sign a few autographs and pose for photographs. I think that one of the reasons the Lisbon Lions are still so popular at these events, aside from being loved for our achievements on the field, is that it is so difficult to get modern-day players to turn up and visit Celtic supporters' clubs. The Lisbon Lions are so respected that everywhere we go we get the 'we are not worthy' treatment and I have to say that sometimes I am a bit embarrassed by that, but the people you meet are so well-intentioned and they do mean it when they tell you how much meeting a Lisbon Lion means to them.

There had been talk of a Lisbon Lions testimonial for years before it finally took place in 2003. We would have liked it to be at the end of the season but I think the arrangements for the testimonial, which saw the 2003 Celtic team take on Feyenoord, were a bit rushed and the match was played in sub-zero temperatures on a winter's evening in the third week in January, just when everyone was completely skint after the excesses of the festive season. There could hardly have been a less attractive date for a testimonial. The punters were rather reluctant to come out but there was a last-minute rush and they had to delay the kick-off for half an hour. Eventually, we got a crowd of 22,000. We had wanted the match to be on 25 May, the anniversary of the European Cup win in Lisbon, but the club said that was impossible. It obviously wasn't because they played the Henrik Larsson benefit game against Sevilla on 25 May 2004 and they even made a point of stating in their advance publicity that the match was being played on the anniversary of us winning the European Cup in Lisbon. If they had arranged our match for 25 May we might not have got a full house of 60,000 but we would have got a helluva lot more than we did get. Nevertheless, it was a good gesture by the club because they were not bound to do anything on our behalf. We didn't make a lot of money from it but we all got a couple of bob and the people who ran it, headed by Willie Haughey, did a tremendous job. It was a smashing occasion, very nostalgic, and I am quite sure that the people who came along to the match enjoyed themselves, even though Feyenoord won.

It was tragic when Ronnie Simpson became the second of the Lisbon Lions to pass away, at the age of 73, in April 2004. Ronnie was a wonderful guy, the oldest by far in our team, and a magnificent goalkeeper. He had a great, dry, droll sense of humour. The rest of us, when we got together, would be competing for the limelight but Ronnie would just sit back quietly and, after a while, come out with a funny remark. He will be sadly missed. We used to kid him about being the oldest among us by saying, 'Come on, "faither", why don't you pop your clogs so that we can see what kind of send-off we will all be getting?' It was just part of the banter between us and Ronnie took it all in good humour. Billy McNeill used to say to me of Ronnie, 'Do you actually think he will go first?' As the oldest he should have done but it turned out to be the youngest of us who went first when Bobby Murdoch sadly passed away in the spring of 2001, aged only 56. We were all really shocked by that, Ronnie in particular. Bobby wasn't really looking after himself by the end of his life but when somebody dies suddenly, as he did, it still takes you by surprise.

A few years ago, Stevie Chalmers was in his garden at home in Bishopbriggs when he suffered the first of three heart attacks that arrived in quick succession. He collapsed at home with the first heart attack and was being rushed to hospital when he suffered the second, at which stage they stabilised him. Inside the hospital, he suffered a third heart attack. Mary and I went up to see him and there were all sorts of tubes attached to him to keep him alive. At his bedside, his wife Sadie and his daughters were there, looking at him lovingly. Then this wee boy came up to me and asked for my autograph. I said, pointing to Stevie, 'I think you'd better get his first, before it's too late.' Shortly afterwards we were in Dublin for a Lisbon Lions function and I bought a huge card for Stevie and got it signed by all the boys. By now he was out of hospital but the card read, 'Fifty ways to say goodbye ... *arrivederci, au revoir* ...' and so on. Thankfully, Stevie has recovered fully.

I still attend football matches although it is a long time since I attended a Scotland match at Hampden Park – not since the '80s. I'll go to nine or ten Celtic games per season. We are guaranteed seats in the Jock Stein Stand. The team wins the vast majority of its matches but the punters are still restless. I think that's because they would like to see Celtic play in a bit more of an 'up and at 'em' style but that is not possible in the modern game because you've got to hold on to the ball at all costs. The top sides in Europe nowadays would rather play the ball twenty yards backwards and keep it than pass it twenty yards forwards and lose it because it is when the ball goes forward that the opposition is more likely to get a chance to intercept it. As I get older, I find that I can be bothered less and less with the enormous amount of traffic that you have to sit in before and after a match at Celtic Park. After a match, it is at least an hour and a half before you can get away from the main car park outside the south stand and, if I am driving, it is not as if I can go for a couple of snifters in the 67 Club to pass the time before heading home. I also go to watch Stirling Albion seven or eight times a season and matches at Forthbank do not present the same problem: you can get a space in the car park seconds before kick-off and be away seconds after the final whistle. I often go without the car, pop into the boardroom for a few drinks, and David drives me back to Dunblane. If I see anything in a game, I sometimes give David or Allan Moore, the head coach, a wee word of advice but whether they want to listen to it is up to them.

In my playing days, I used to get a hard time from the Rangers fans because I was a Protestant. They would single me out for special privileges, you might say, before, during and after the games between Celtic and Rangers. They would call me a 'turncoat bastard' and so on. I don't go near Ibrox now for Old Firm matches although I go to the games at Celtic Park because I know I can drive into the car park and go straight to my seat without any problems. The last time I went to Ibrox as a spectator, about two years ago, Rangers fans called me all the names under the sun, spitting at me and throwing coins at me. It also happened once at Celtic Park, about five years ago. I left the game ten minutes early and found that the Rangers supporters were also coming out early because Celtic were winning. I had wanted to get away sharpish and, stupidly, had arranged for Mary to pick me up in London Road ten minutes before the end of the game. I went down to the pre-arranged meeting spot just as the Rangers supporters were coming along from the Rangers end and the dog's abuse that I got was incredible, obnoxious in the extreme. They were spitting, shouting at me, throwing coins, making blasphemous remarks in my direction – and there was nothing I could do. There were police about but they just turn their heads, don't they?

I have never been bigoted in my life and I have no time for bigotry at all. I have seen it first-hand from both sides and I honestly think that the Rangers bigots are ten times worse than the Celtic bigots. There is bad blood on both sides but the Rangers bigots, for some reason, are more vicious.

There are also hooligans in Dunblane, as there are hooligans everywhere else. Not everyone in Dunblane is as squeaky clean as you might imagine. A car of mine was scraped with a nail on the day after I had bought it. There were a dozen other cars parked in the same street so the only reason I can think of for that happening is that I am an ex-Celtic footballer.

I was not surprised to watch my former Nottingham Forest team-mate Martin O'Neill's career unfold. He went on to become a very good player for Forest and to win 64 caps for Northern Ireland. He was always very single-minded and let you know he was on the park; even as a teenager he wasn't a shy wee boy. There was also a touch of Irish temper in the mix. Those qualities helped him to become a successful manager of Wycombe Wanderers and Leicester City, where teamwork was to the fore, and when he arrived at Celtic Park it was shown clearly from early on that teamwork is the major strength of any side he fields, allied to fitness and ability. Throughout his managerial career he has always concentrated on fielding guys who will play for each other and there is no reason why he should change his ways because he has been successful at all the clubs he has managed.

I have met Martin a few times since he came to Scotland; it was great to see him again when he came to Celtic as manager in the summer of 2000. I gave him a couple of days to settle in and then went into Celtic Park to say hello and wish him all the very best. We had a chat about Celtic and I said to him, 'There are only three things you need to do.' He said, 'What are they?' I said, 'Beat Rangers.' He said, 'What are the other two?' I said, 'No, that's it:

beat Rangers, three times. If you beat Rangers three times in the League, you have won it. You will have won nine points and they will have lost nine points so there will be an eighteen-point gap and all the other League matches will fall into place for you.' I don't think he quite understood the intensity of the Old Firm rivalry when he first arrived but he knows now. Martin also took the Lisbon Lions out for dinner in the close season of the first couple of years after he became manager and paid for the lot himself. He loved the company and I think he was maybe also trying to pick our brains to get a few ideas on how we had all got on together and how we were able to get the teamwork going.

I don't think Martin would suffer fools gladly. He is deep; he gives nothing away. He will not volunteer any information. If you ask him a question and he wants to answer it, he will, but if it is one he doesn't want to answer he will hedge and dodge around it. He plays everything very close to his chest. He is very shrewd and John Robertson and Steve Walford form a good team along with him.

My aim for the future is just to keep plugging away with my work as a financial adviser and eventually reduce my working week from five days to two or three. As long as I am fit, I will be able to do this job until the day I drop because it is essentially about communicating with people and solving problems for them, so I am in the fortunate position that if I work quite smartly, I can obtain a reasonable income from two or three days' work per week. That would allow me to slow down a bit, rest the bones and do some more fishing and reading. I enjoy books by John le Carré and Robert Ludlum and football books such as Sir Alex Ferguson's autobiography.

When I get home from a day's fishing, Mary will say to me, 'How was your day?' I'll say, 'Brilliant.' She'll say, 'What did you catch?' Sometimes I'll reply, 'Nothing.' She'll say, 'How can your day have been brilliant if you didn't catch any fish?' That does puzzle people, but you concentrate so much on trying to catch fish that you forget time and that makes it incredibly relaxing. People think it's boring but it's only boring if you don't know what you're doing. You are never guaranteed to catch anything when you go fishing but you are guaranteed to have a good time. We go fishing in threes up at our own fishing-club loch in Callander, which is absolutely fantastic. We take a catering bag packed with sandwiches and bottles of wine and have a wonderful day out. You can come back soaked but you will have enjoyed a superb day. Mary has even been enticed to come along occasionally. On the first day I took her, it was the day after we had stocked the loch with trout, but she didn't know that. After about half an hour she had caught three fish and thought she was the greatest fisherman in the world. She didn't know that we had put 500 fish in the loch the day before.

I try to do a day's fishing once a month and that clears the brain, gets you out of the office and stops you thinking about business. I still do the odd bit of shooting and hunting near Dunblane and the occasional charity clay-pigeon shoot at Dunkeld and Gleneagles.

I have slowed down a bit in recent years – my body has told me to do that. I now drive a Chrysler Neon, which is a very comfortable car, but far removed from the flash days of the S-Type Jaguar. Joining Celtic in 1961 widened my horizons to an enormous degree and made the introverted boy from Craigneuk into an extrovert but nowadays I am halfway between introvert and extrovert. I am now, dare I say it, a bit more sensible. I don't have money to throw around because I never earned a fortune from playing football. Mary and I may not have a lot of money in the bank but we have a good lifestyle. We eat well, like a glass of wine and take three or four holidays a year. Dunblane is a beautiful small town with a couple of good pubs and equally handy for travelling from central Scotland to Glasgow or going north or to Edinburgh.

I had had no association with the managing or coaching side of football after finishing with Albion Rovers until Hogmanay 2003, when my son David, in his capacity as assistant coach at Stirling Albion, asked me to take the players through a training session. The idea was to give them a change of routine midway through the season and ease the pain of reporting for duty during the festive period. I took them through an hour-and-a-half session and made sure there was a lot of fun in it. They thoroughly enjoyed it and afterwards David and Allan Moore asked me back again but

I had no interest in making it anything more than a one-off and I told them so.

I wouldn't change anything about my life and I regret nothing I have done. One or two incidents in my playing career do still rankle, though, even at this distance. Jock Stein's refusal to contemplate my leaving Celtic for Barcelona was a big disappointment. My other major bugbear was my exit from Celtic in 1971 because, deep down, I never wanted to leave the club. Then again, if I hadn't left when I did I might never have tasted English football or have led Dundee to the League Cup. I would probably never have had the experience of being manager of Dundee, and it was when I was on holiday from Dundee, in Majorca, that I met Mary. I am a great believer in things falling into place. I don't think we manage to plan too many of the things that happen to us. It is impossible to ignore coincidence and fate; so many things in life just fall into or out of place through circumstances over which we have no control. You can still make your own luck in life by working hard and keeping a smile on your face. If you do that, then, like me, you are sure to get a rub of the green.

INDEX